Table of Contents

As Easy as 1–2–3

 1 **Prepare** the assessment task activity.

2 **Administer** the task and record the student's performance.

3 **Reteach** or provide additional practice using the reproducible activity sheet.

Everything You Need

Each assessment task includes:

- **Scripted instructions**
  for administering the assessment task

- **Full-color mats and cards**
  to engage the student in a specific task

- **Class checklist**
  to record each student's performance

- **Reproducible activity sheets**
  for additional skill practice

When to Conduct an Assessment

You may choose to use assessment tasks in any of the following ways:

- Assess students at the beginning of the school year to determine individual student skill levels.

- Administer an assessment after a specific skill has been taught to help confirm mastery or need for further instruction.

- Assess students throughout the year to monitor progress. Use the correlation chart on page 6 to correlate assessments with your lesson plans.

You may also wish to visit www.teaching-standards.com to view how the skills are correlated to your state's standards.

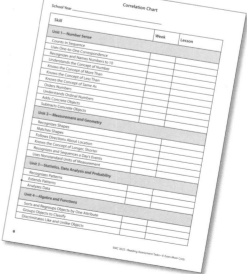

Preparing an Assessment Task Activity

Assemble each assessment task activity and place it in an envelope. Store the envelopes in a file box or crate for easy access.

Materials:
- 9" x 12" (23 x 30.5 cm) large manila envelopes
- scissors
- clear tape
- scripted instructions, manipulatives, class checklist, and activity sheet for the specific assessment task

Steps to Follow:
1. Remove and laminate the *scripted instruction page*. Tape it to the front of the envelope.
2. Remove and laminate the *manipulatives* (sorting mats, task cards, etc.). Store cards in a smaller envelope or plastic bag.
3. Reproduce the *class checklist*. Tape it to the back of the envelope.
4. Make multiple copies of the *activity sheet* and store them in the envelope.

Make one copy of the *Individual Student Assessment Checklist* (page 5) for each student in your class. You may wish to keep these checklists in a separate binder so they are easily referenced.

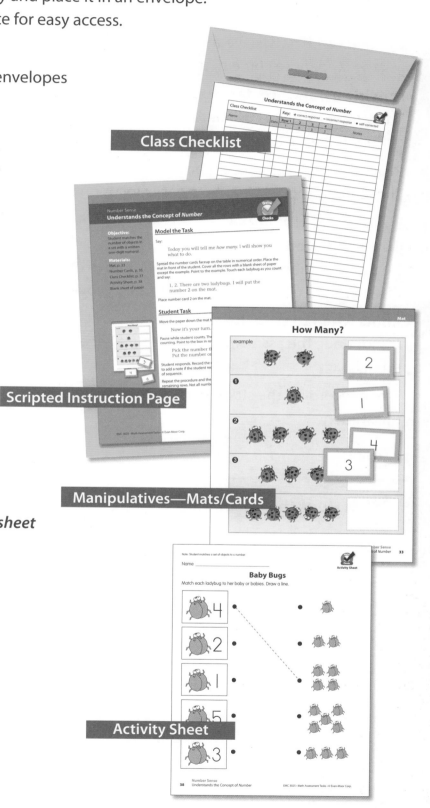

Class Checklist

Scripted Instruction Page

Manipulatives—Mats/Cards

Activity Sheet

How to Conduct an Assessment

- **Be prepared.**
  Preread the scripted instructions. Follow the directions at the top of the script for setting out the cards and mats. Have the class checklist at hand to record the student's responses. Do not ask the student to come to the table until all task materials are in place.

- **Provide a non-threatening atmosphere.**
  The student should complete the task at a quiet, isolated table. Refer to the activity as a "task" or "job," not as a "test."

- **Provide a non-distracting environment.**
  The student should be able to easily focus on the task. Sit next to the student. Communicate in a clear, concise way.

- **Be an unbiased assessor.**
  Do not encourage or discourage or approve or disapprove of the student's responses. Be careful not to use facial expressions that provide feedback.

- **Know when to stop the assessment.**
  Discontinue the assessment activity if it becomes obvious that the student cannot do the task.

- **Be discreet.**
  When recording the student's responses, keep the checklist close to you so it will not distract the student.

What does this mean?

Auditory Only

Some tasks are auditory only, and are indicated by this icon on the teacher script page. Auditory tasks do not contain mats or task cards.

EMC 3026 • Math Assessment Tasks • © Evan-Moor Corp.

Individual Student Assessment Checklist

Name _____   School Year _____

Skill	Dates Tested	Date Mastered
Unit 1—Number Sense		
Compares Sets		
Counts to 15		
Counts to 30		
Counts Objects		
Recognizes and Names Numbers 1 to 15		
Recognizes and Names Numbers 16 to 30		
Orders Numbers 1 to 15		
Orders Numbers 16 to 30		
Knows the Concept *More, Less*		
Adds Using Manipulatives		
Subtracts Using Manipulatives		
Makes Reasonable Estimates		
Unit 2—Measurement and Geometry		
Compares Objects by Length		
Compares Objects by Weight		
Compares Objects by Capacity		
Names the Days of the Week		
Identifies the Time of Events		
Names and Identifies Plane Shapes		
Compares Plane and Solid Shapes		
Unit 3—Statistics, Data Analysis, and Probability		
Records Data on a Graph		
Describes and Extends Simple Patterns		
Unit 4—Algebra and Functions		
Sorts and Classifies Objects		
Identifies and Classifies Objects		

Correlation Chart

School Year _____

Skill	Week	Lesson
Unit 1—Number Sense		
Compares Sets		
Counts to 15		
Counts to 30		
Counts Objects		
Recognizes and Names Numbers 1 to 15		
Recognizes and Names Numbers 16 to 30		
Orders Numbers 1 to 15		
Orders Numbers 16 to 30		
Knows the Concept *More, Less*		
Adds Using Manipulatives		
Subtracts Using Manipulatives		
Makes Reasonable Estimates		
Unit 2—Measurement and Geometry		
Compares Objects by Length		
Compares Objects by Weight		
Compares Objects by Capacity		
Names the Days of the Week		
Identifies the Time of Events		
Names and Identifies Plane Shapes		
Compares Plane and Solid Shapes		
Unit 3—Statistics, Data Analysis, and Probability		
Records Data on a Graph		
Describes and Extends Simple Patterns		
Unit 4—Algebra and Functions		
Sorts and Classifies Objects		
Identifies and Classifies Objects		

Checks

Unit 1
Number Sense

Objective:
Student compares sets of objects using the terms *more, same,* and *less.*

Materials:

Blue Mat, p. 11

Green Mat, p. 13

Apple Cards, p. 15

Class Checklist, p. 17

Activity Sheet, p. 18

Blank sheet of paper

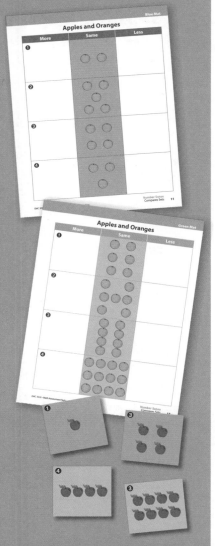

Student Task

(Note: You may adjust this task to the abilities of your students. Use one or both mats. The blue mat is less challenging than the green mat.)

Say:

> Today you will compare apples and oranges.

Use the same color mat and cards. Place the mat in front of the student. Cover all the rows except for row 1 with a blank sheet of paper. Move card 1 along each section of row 1 as you say:

> Are there more apples than oranges, the same number, or less?

Student responds. Place card 1 on row 1, indicating the student's response. Move the paper down the mat to reveal row 2. Move card 2 along each section of row 2 as you say:

> Are there more apples than oranges, the same number, or less?

Student responds. Place card 2 on row 2, indicating the student's response.

Repeat the procedure and the script modeled above for rows 3 and 4. Use the mat as a reference to record the student's responses on the class checklist.

Apples and Oranges

More	Same	Less
1		
2		
3		
4		

Number Sense
Compares Sets   **11**

Compares Sets

Number Sense

EMC 3026 • © Evan-Moor Corp.

Apples and Oranges

More	Same	Less
❶		
❷		
❸		
❹		

Number Sense
Compares Sets   **13**

Compares Sets

Number Sense

EMC 3026 • © Evan-Moor Corp.

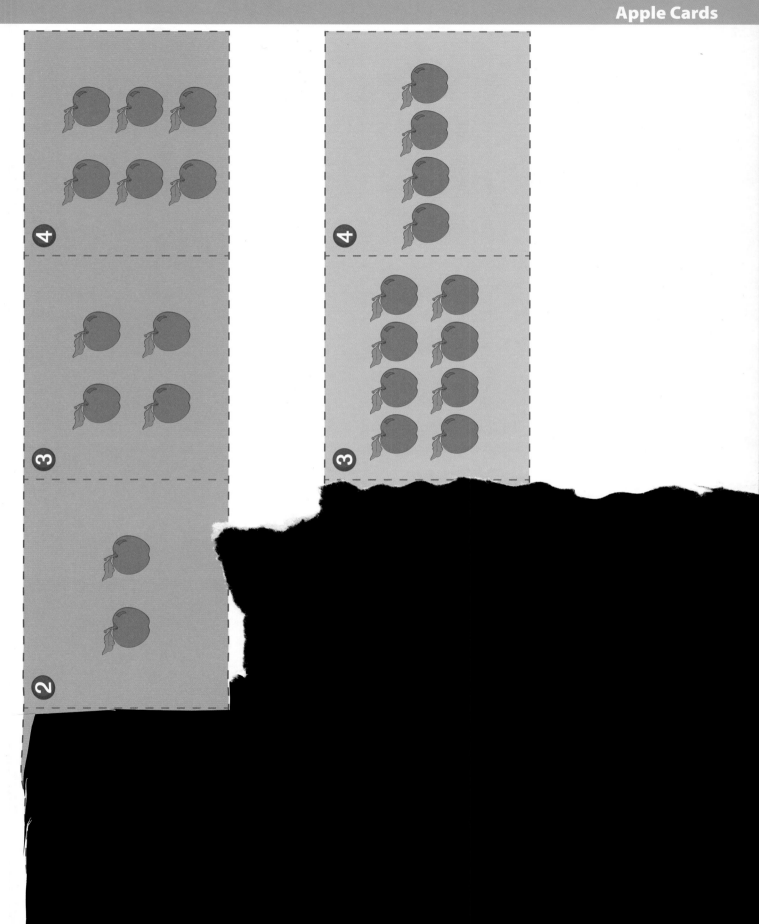

Compares Sets
Number Sense

Compares Sets
Number Sense

Compares Sets
Number Sense

Compares Sets
Number Sense

Compares Sets
Number Sense

Compares Sets

Class Checklist		Key: + correct response − incorrect response ● self-corrected							
Name	**Date**	**Blue Mat**				**Green Mat**			**Notes**
		Less	Less	Same	More	Less	Same	More	Less	

Note: Student compares sets.

Name _____

Less and More

Circle the correct answer.

❶ Which has more?

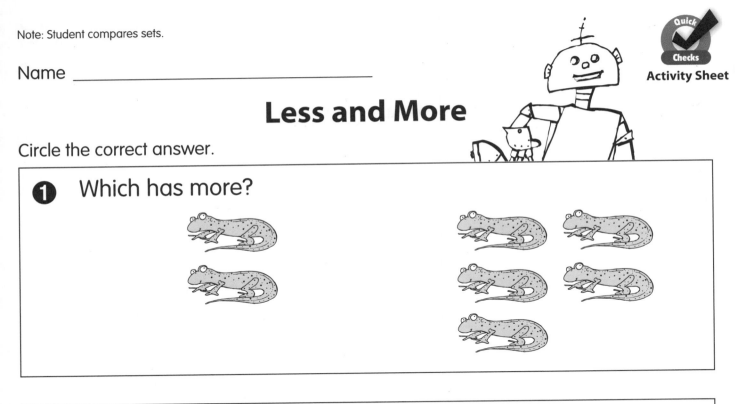

❷ Which has less?

❸ Which has more?

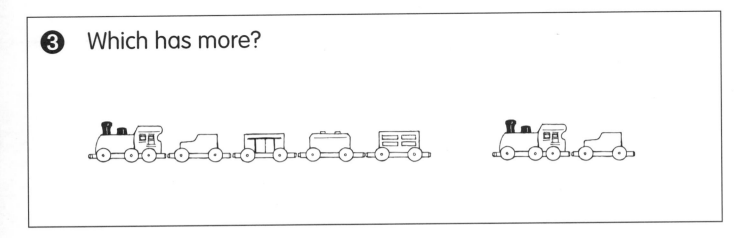

Number Sense
Compares Sets

Objective:
Student counts orally from 1 to 15.

Materials:
Class Checklist, p. 21

Activity Sheet, p. 22

Auditory Only

Student Task

Say:

> Today you will count to 15 for me. Let's begin. Start with 1.

Student responds. Record how far the student counted accurately on the class checklist. Use the **Notes** column to indicate the numbers the student missed, reversed, confused, and so on.

Counts to 15

Class Checklist	Record how high the student counts accurately to 15.		
Name	Date	1 to 15	Notes

Note: Student counts to 15.

Name _____

A School of Fish

Trace the numbers. Count out loud.

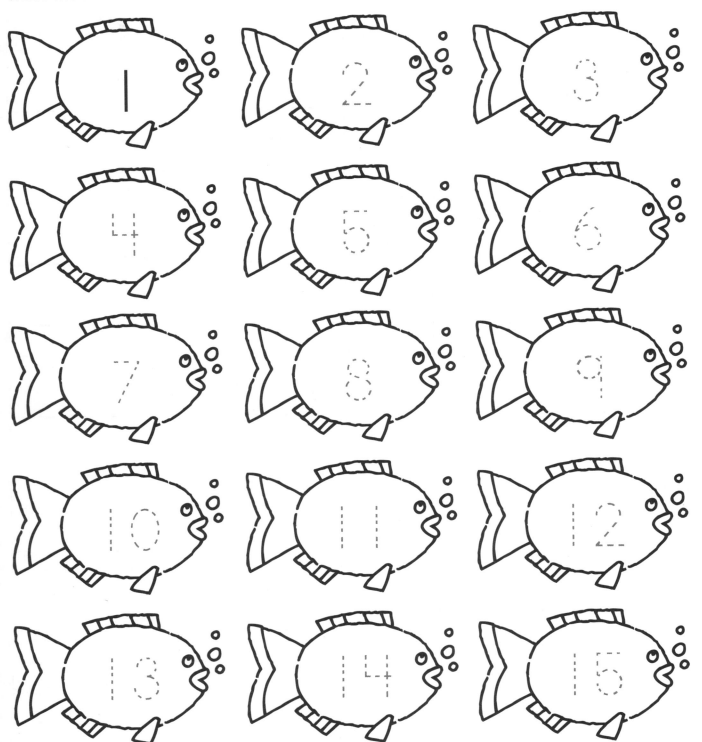

Objective:
Student counts orally from 1 to 30.

Materials:
Class Checklist, p. 25

Activity Sheet, p. 26

Auditory Only

Student Task

Say:

> Today you will count to 30 for me. Let's begin. Start with 1.

Student responds. Record how far the student counted accurately on the class checklist. Use the **Notes** column to indicate the numbers the student missed, reversed, confused, and so on.

EMC 3026 • Math Assessment Tasks • © Evan-Moor Corp.

Counts to 30

Class Checklist	Record how high the student counts accurately to 30.		
Name	Date	1 to 30	Notes

Name _____

Make a Bank

Connect the dots. Count out loud. Start with **1**.

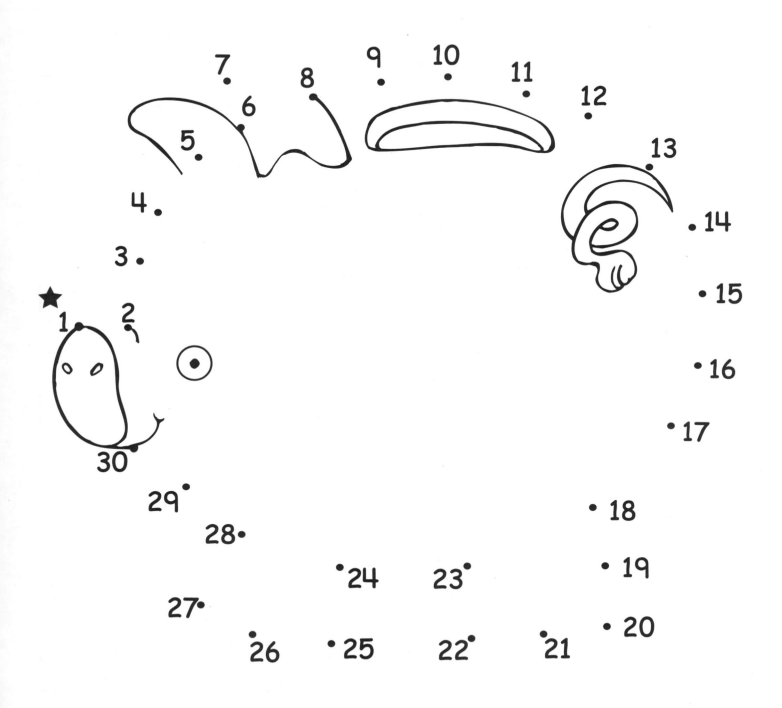

Quick Checks

Objective:
Student counts manipulatives using one-to-one correspondence.

Materials:
Mat, p. 29

Picture Cards, p. 31

Class Checklist, p. 33

Activity Sheet, p. 34

Student Task

(Note: You may adjust this task to suit the abilities of your students.)

Say:

> Today you will count things for me.

Place the fish picture cards faceup in a pile on the table. Place the fishbowl mat in front of the student. Say:

> Let's begin. Put four fish in the bowl. Count each fish as you put it in the bowl.

Student responds. Record the student's response on the class checklist. Clear the mat. Say:

> Now put six fish in the bowl. Count each fish as you put it in the bowl.

Record the student's response.

EMC 3026 • Math Assessment Tasks • © Evan-Moor Corp.

Counting

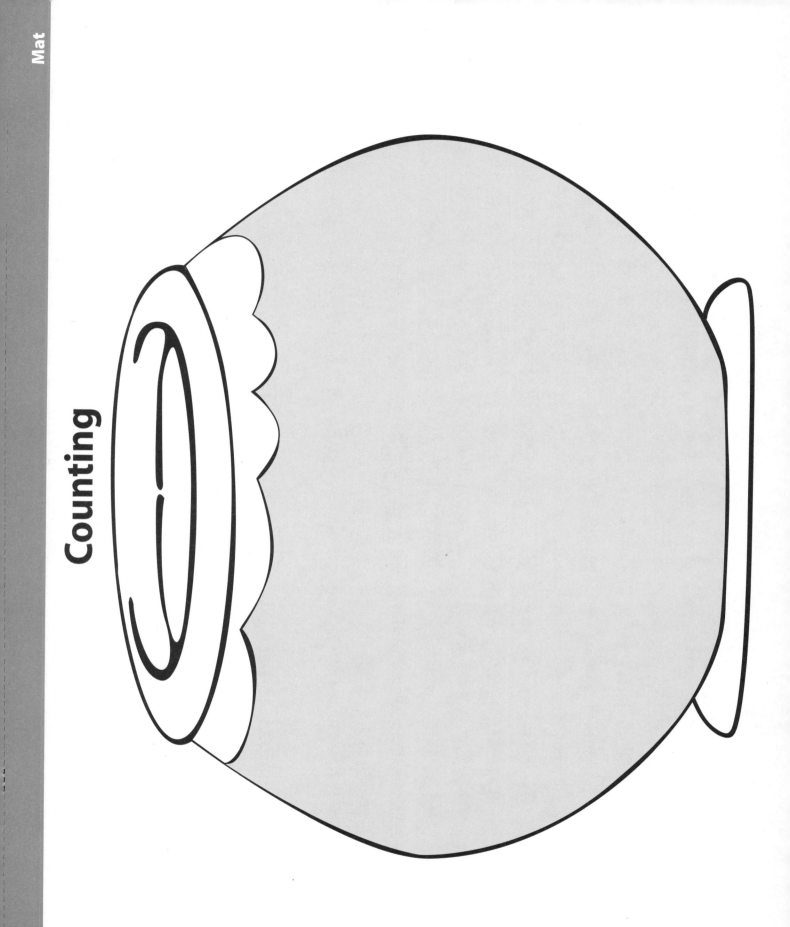

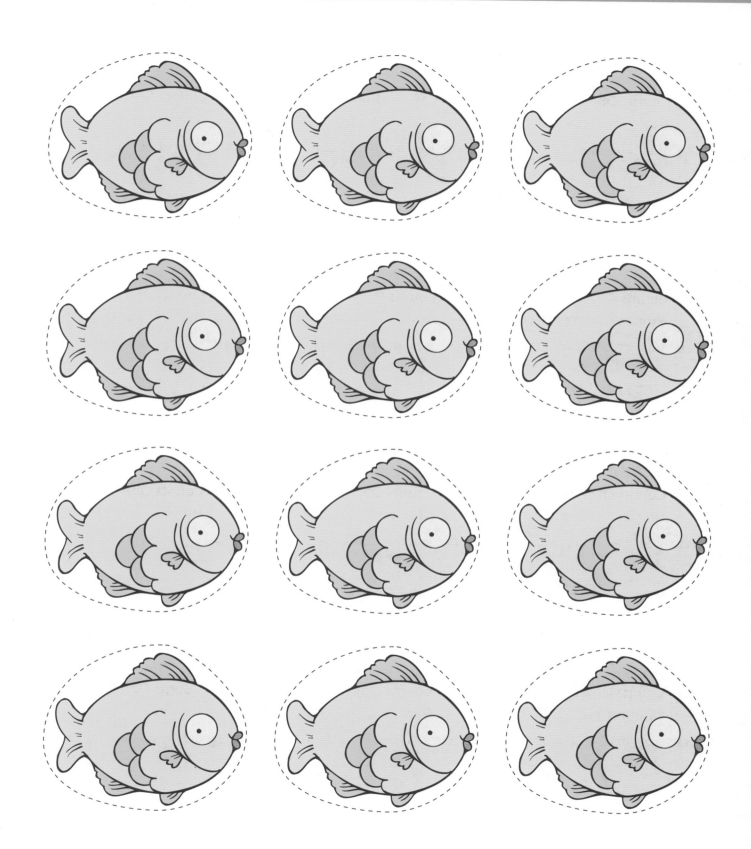

Counts Objects

Number Sense

EMC 3026 • © Evan-Moor Corp.

Counts Objects

Number Sense

EMC 3026 • © Evan-Moor Corp.

Counts Objects

Number Sense

EMC 3026 • © Evan-Moor Corp.

Counts Objects

Number Sense

EMC 3026 • © Evan-Moor Corp.

Counts Objects

Number Sense

EMC 3026 • © Evan-Moor Corp.

Counts Objects

Number Sense

EMC 3026 • © Evan-Moor Corp.

Counts Objects

Number Sense

EMC 3026 • © Evan-Moor Corp.

Counts Objects

Number Sense

EMC 3026 • © Evan-Moor Corp.

Counts Objects

Number Sense

EMC 3026 • © Evan-Moor Corp.

Counts Objects

Number Sense

EMC 3026 • © Evan-Moor Corp.

Counts Objects

Number Sense

EMC 3026 • © Evan-Moor Corp.

Counts Objects

Number Sense

EMC 3026 • © Evan-Moor Corp.

Counts Objects

Class Checklist	Key:	+ correct response	− incorrect response	● self-corrected
Name	Date	Four Fish	Six Fish	Notes

Note: Student counts objects.

Name _____

Bugs, Bugs, Bugs

Cut out the bugs. Put the bugs on the pictures. Count out loud.

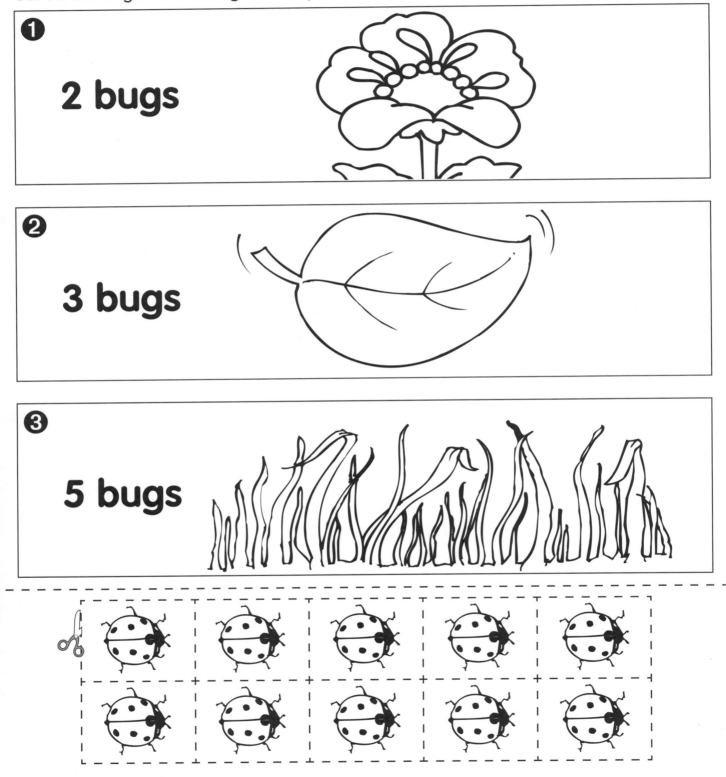

1 2 bugs

2 3 bugs

3 5 bugs

Recognizes and Names Numbers 1 to 15

Quick
Checks

Objective:

Student recognizes and orally names numbers 1 through 15.

Materials:

Number Cards, p. 37

Class Checklist, p. 39

Activity Sheet, p. 40

Student Task

Say:

> Today I will show you some cards. You will read the numbers.

Hold the cards in random order. Show the first card to the student. Say:

> Let's begin. What is this number?

Student responds.

Use the **Notes** column on the class checklist for recording the responses:
   Make a **+** if all the numbers are read correctly.
   List each number that is named incorrectly.
   For numbers that are self-corrected, make a • followed by the number.

Show the remaining 14 number cards and record each response.

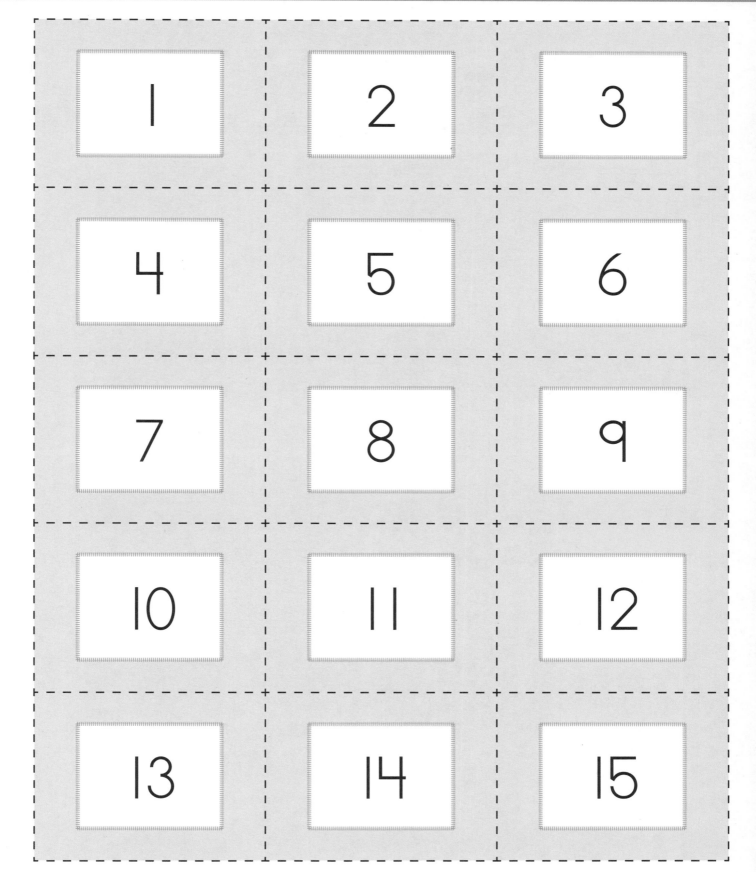

1	2	3
4	5	6
7	8	9
10	11	12
13	14	15

Number Sense
Recognizes and Names Numbers 1 to 15

**Recognizes and Names
Numbers 1 to 15**

Number Sense

EMC 3026 • © Evan-Moor Corp.

**Recognizes and Names
Numbers 1 to 15**

Number Sense

EMC 3026 • © Evan-Moor Corp.

**Recognizes and Names
Numbers 1 to 15**

Number Sense

EMC 3026 • © Evan-Moor Corp.

**Recognizes and Names
Numbers 1 to 15**

Number Sense

EMC 3026 • © Evan-Moor Corp.

**Recognizes and Names
Numbers 1 to 15**

Number Sense

EMC 3026 • © Evan-Moor Corp.

**Recognizes and Names
Numbers 1 to 15**

Number Sense

EMC 3026 • © Evan-Moor Corp.

**Recognizes and Names
Numbers 1 to 15**

Number Sense

EMC 3026 • © Evan-Moor Corp.

**Recognizes and Names
Numbers 1 to 15**

Number Sense

EMC 3026 • © Evan-Moor Corp.

**Recognizes and Names
Numbers 1 to 15**

Number Sense

EMC 3026 • © Evan-Moor Corp.

**Recognizes and Names
Numbers 1 to 15**

Number Sense

EMC 3026 • © Evan-Moor Corp.

**Recognizes and Names
Numbers 1 to 15**

Number Sense

EMC 3026 • © Evan-Moor Corp.

**Recognizes and Names
Numbers 1 to 15**

Number Sense

EMC 3026 • © Evan-Moor Corp.

**Recognizes and Names
Numbers 1 to 15**

Number Sense

EMC 3026 • © Evan-Moor Corp.

**Recognizes and Names
Numbers 1 to 15**

Number Sense

EMC 3026 • © Evan-Moor Corp.

**Recognizes and Names
Numbers 1 to 15**

Number Sense

EMC 3026 • © Evan-Moor Corp.

Recognizes and Names Numbers 1 to 15

Class Checklist	Key: **+** all correct ● List each self-corrected number. List each incorrectly named number.	
Name	Date	Notes

Note: Student names numbers 1 to 15.

Name _____

Name the Numbers

Read the numbers out loud.

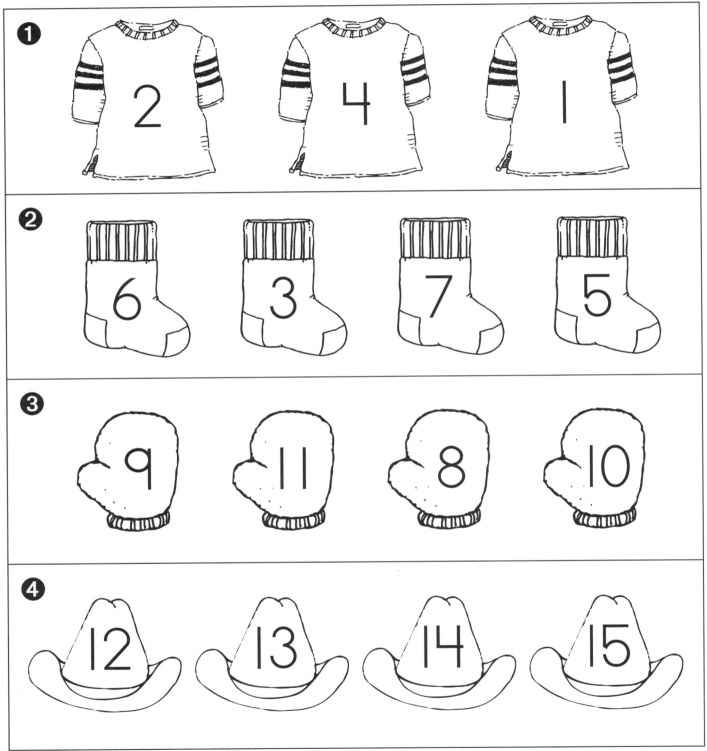

Objective:
Student recognizes and orally names numbers 16 through 30.

Materials:
Number Cards, p. 43

Class Checklist, p. 45

Activity Sheet, p. 46

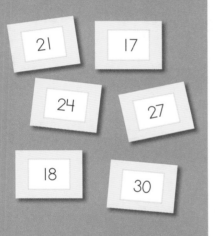

Student Task

Say:

> Today I will show you some cards. You will read the numbers.

Hold the cards in random order. Show the first card to the student. Say:

> Let's begin. What is this number?

Student responds.

Use the **Notes** column on the class checklist for recording the responses:

   Make a **+** if all the numbers are read correctly.

   List each number that is named incorrectly.

   For numbers that are self-corrected, make a • followed by the number.

Show the remaining 14 number cards and record each response.

16 17 18

19 20 21

22 23 24

25 26 27

28 29 30

Number Sense
Recognizes and Names Numbers 16 to 30 **43**

Recognizes and Names
Numbers 16 to 30

Number Sense

EMC 3026 • © Evan-Moor Corp.

Recognizes and Names
Numbers 16 to 30

Number Sense

EMC 3026 • © Evan-Moor Corp.

Recognizes and Names
Numbers 16 to 30

Number Sense

EMC 3026 • © Evan-Moor Corp.

Recognizes and Names
Numbers 16 to 30

Number Sense

EMC 3026 • © Evan-Moor Corp.

Recognizes and Names
Numbers 16 to 30

Number Sense

EMC 3026 • © Evan-Moor Corp.

Recognizes and Names
Numbers 16 to 30

Number Sense

EMC 3026 • © Evan-Moor Corp.

Recognizes and Names
Numbers 16 to 30

Number Sense

EMC 3026 • © Evan-Moor Corp.

Recognizes and Names
Numbers 16 to 30

Number Sense

EMC 3026 • © Evan-Moor Corp.

Recognizes and Names
Numbers 16 to 30

Number Sense

EMC 3026 • © Evan-Moor Corp.

Recognizes and Names
Numbers 16 to 30

Number Sense

EMC 3026 • © Evan-Moor Corp.

Recognizes and Names
Numbers 16 to 30

Number Sense

EMC 3026 • © Evan-Moor Corp.

Recognizes and Names
Numbers 16 to 30

Number Sense

EMC 3026 • © Evan-Moor Corp.

Recognizes and Names
Numbers 16 to 30

Number Sense

EMC 3026 • © Evan-Moor Corp.

Recognizes and Names
Numbers 16 to 30

Number Sense

EMC 3026 • © Evan-Moor Corp.

Recognizes and Names
Numbers 16 to 30

Number Sense

EMC 3026 • © Evan-Moor Corp.

Recognizes and Names Numbers 16 to 30

Class Checklist	Key:	+ all correct ● List each self-corrected number. List each incorrectly named number.
Name	**Date**	**Notes**

Name _____

Funny Fish

Read the numbers out loud.

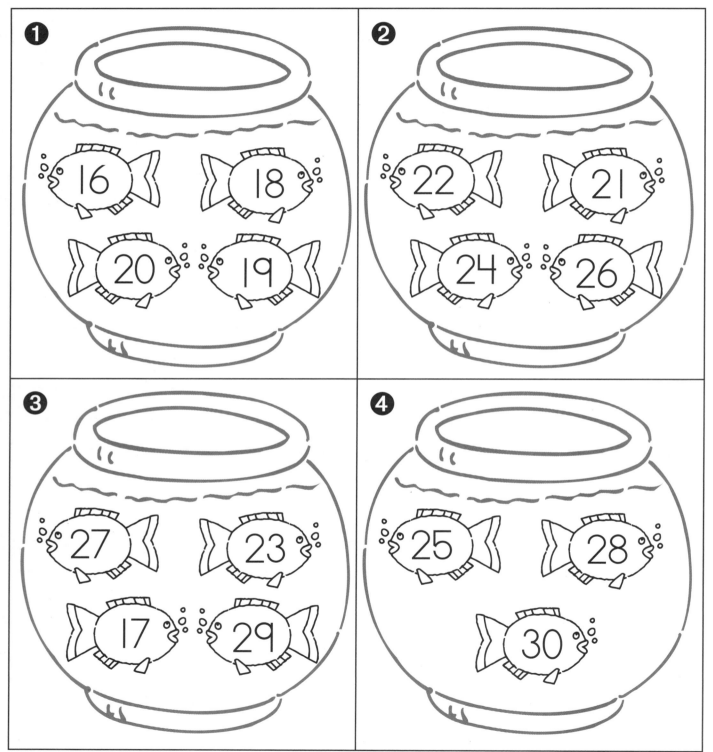

Student Task

Say:

> Today you will put numbers in order from the smallest to the largest.

Arrange the number cards in rows on the table. Place the cards faceup in random order. Place card 1, the engine, in front of the student. Say:

> Let's begin. You will make a train. Put the train card that comes after the number 1 on the table.

Student responds. Say:

> Put the number that comes next.

Student responds. Say:

> Now put the rest of the cards in order.

Student responds. Use the completed train as a reference to record the student's responses on the class checklist.

Objective:
Student orders one- and two-digit numbers from smallest to largest.

Materials:
Number Cards, p. 49

Class Checklist, p. 51

Activity Sheet, p. 52

Orders Numbers 1 to 15

Number Sense

EMC 3026 • © Evan-Moor Corp.

Orders Numbers 1 to 15

Number Sense

EMC 3026 • © Evan-Moor Corp.

Orders Numbers 1 to 15

Number Sense

EMC 3026 • © Evan-Moor Corp.

Orders Numbers 1 to 15

Number Sense

EMC 3026 • © Evan-Moor Corp.

Orders Numbers 1 to 15

Number Sense

EMC 3026 • © Evan-Moor Corp.

Orders Numbers 1 to 15

Number Sense

EMC 3026 • © Evan-Moor Corp.

Orders Numbers 1 to 15

Number Sense

EMC 3026 • © Evan-Moor Corp.

Orders Numbers 1 to 15

Number Sense

EMC 3026 • © Evan-Moor Corp.

Orders Numbers 1 to 15

Number Sense

EMC 3026 • © Evan-Moor Corp.

Orders Numbers 1 to 15

Number Sense

EMC 3026 • © Evan-Moor Corp.

Orders Numbers 1 to 15

Number Sense

EMC 3026 • © Evan-Moor Corp.

Orders Numbers 1 to 15

Number Sense

EMC 3026 • © Evan-Moor Corp.

Orders Numbers 1 to 15

Number Sense

EMC 3026 • © Evan-Moor Corp.

Orders Numbers 1 to 15

Number Sense

EMC 3026 • © Evan-Moor Corp.

Orders Numbers 1 to 15

Number Sense

EMC 3026 • © Evan-Moor Corp.

Orders Numbers 1 to 15

Class Checklist		Key: + all correct • List each self-corrected number. List each incorrectly named number.
Name	Date	Notes

Name _____

Wiggle Worms

Cut out the numbers. Glue them in order.

Quick Checks

Objective:
Student orders two-digit numbers from smallest to largest.

Materials:
Number Cards, p. 55

Class Checklist, p. 57

Activity Sheet, p. 58

Student Task

Say:

> Today you will put numbers in order from the smallest to the largest.

Arrange the number cards in rows on the table. Place the cards faceup in random order. Place card 16, the caterpillar's head, on the table in front of the student. Say:

> Let's begin. You will make a caterpillar. Put the card that comes after the number 16 on the table.

Student responds. Say:

> Put the number that comes next.

Student responds. Say:

> Now put the rest of the cards in order.

Student responds. Use the completed caterpillar as a reference to record the student's responses on the class checklist.

Number Sense
Orders Numbers 16 to 30   **55**

Orders Numbers **16 to 30** **Number Sense** EMC 3026 • © Evan-Moor Corp.	**Orders Numbers** **16 to 30** **Number Sense** EMC 3026 • © Evan-Moor Corp.	**Orders Numbers** **16 to 30** **Number Sense** EMC 3026 • © Evan-Moor Corp.
Orders Numbers **16 to 30** **Number Sense** EMC 3026 • © Evan-Moor Corp.	**Orders Numbers** **16 to 30** **Number Sense** EMC 3026 • © Evan-Moor Corp.	**Orders Numbers** **16 to 30** **Number Sense** EMC 3026 • © Evan-Moor Corp.
Orders Numbers **16 to 30** **Number Sense** EMC 3026 • © Evan-Moor Corp.	**Orders Numbers** **16 to 30** **Number Sense** EMC 3026 • © Evan-Moor Corp.	**Orders Numbers** **16 to 30** **Number Sense** EMC 3026 • © Evan-Moor Corp.
Orders Numbers **16 to 30** **Number Sense** EMC 3026 • © Evan-Moor Corp.	**Orders Numbers** **16 to 30** **Number Sense** EMC 3026 • © Evan-Moor Corp.	**Orders Numbers** **16 to 30** **Number Sense** EMC 3026 • © Evan-Moor Corp.
Orders Numbers **16 to 30** **Number Sense** EMC 3026 • © Evan-Moor Corp.	**Orders Numbers** **16 to 30** **Number Sense** EMC 3026 • © Evan-Moor Corp.	**Orders Numbers** **16 to 30** **Number Sense** EMC 3026 • © Evan-Moor Corp.

Number Sense
Orders Numbers 16 to 30

56

EMC 3026 • Math Assessment Tasks • © Evan-Moor Corp.

Orders Numbers 16 to 30

Class Checklist	Key:	+ all correct • List each self-corrected number. List each incorrectly named number.
Name	Date	Notes

Name _____

Make a Garden

Cut out the numbers. Glue them where they belong.

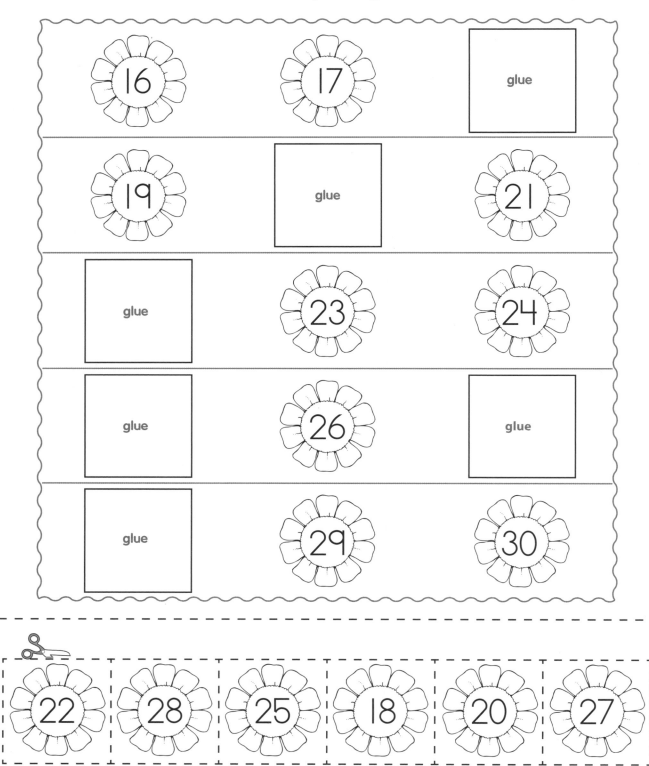

Quick Checks

Objective:
Student compares sets of objects using the terms *more* and *less*.

Materials:
Mat, p. 61

Class Checklist, p. 63

Activity Sheet, p. 64

Blank sheet of paper

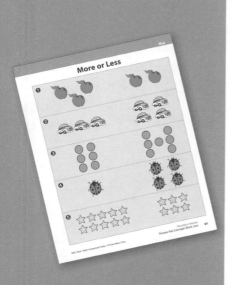

Student Task

Say:

> Today you will look at sets of pictures. You will say which set has more and which set has less.

Place the mat on the table. Cover all the rows except for row 1 with a blank sheet of paper. Say:

> Let's begin. Look at the two sets of apples. Point to the set that has *more*.

Student responds. Record the student's response on the class checklist. Move the paper down the mat to reveal row 2. Say:

> Look at the two sets of cars. Point to the set that has *less*.

Record the response. Reveal row 3. Say:

> Look at the two sets of circles. Point to the set that has *more*.

Record the response. Reveal row 4. Say:

> Look at the two sets of ladybugs. Point to the set that has *less*.

Record the response. Show row 5. Say:

> Look at the two sets of stars. Point to the set that has *more*.

Record the response.

More or Less

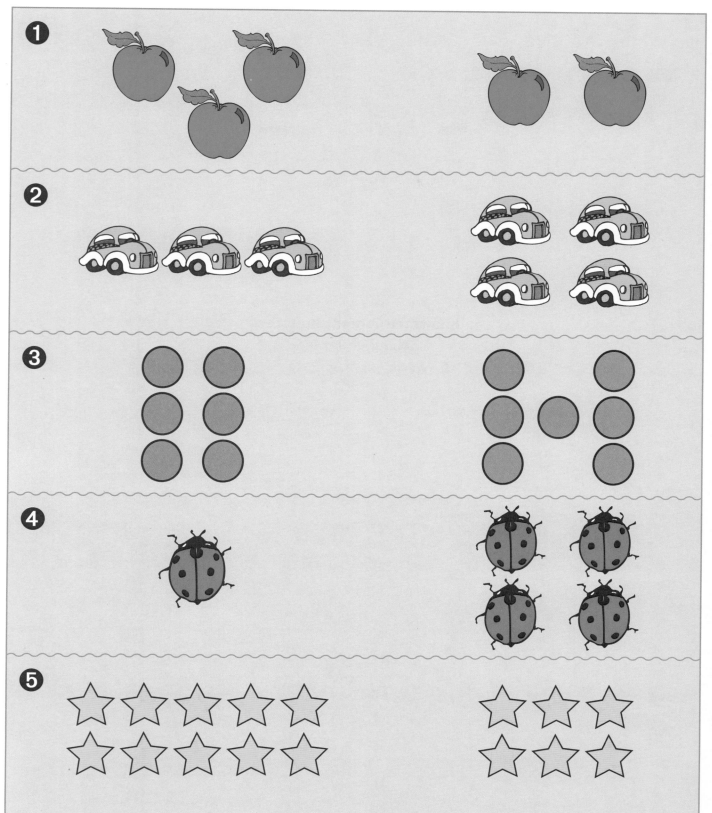

Knows the Concept *More, Less*

Number Sense

EMC 3026 • © Evan-Moor Corp.

Knows the Concept *More, Less*

Class Checklist		**Key:**	+ correct response	− incorrect response	● self-corrected		
Name	Date	Row 1	2	3	4	5	Notes
		3 apples	3 cars	7 circles	1 ladybug	10 stars	

Name _____

More or Less?

Circle the correct picture.

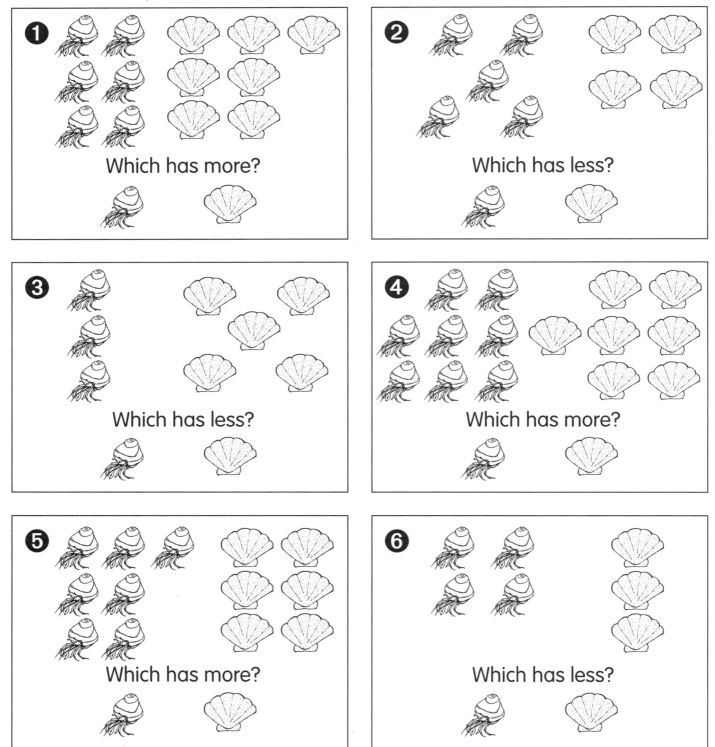

Adds Using Manipulatives

Quick Checks

Objective:
Student uses concrete objects to add one-digit numbers.

Materials:
Student Mat, p. 67

Teacher Mat, p. 69

Counters, p. 69
(or you may use beans)

Class Checklist, p. 71

Activity Sheet, p. 72

Blank sheet of paper

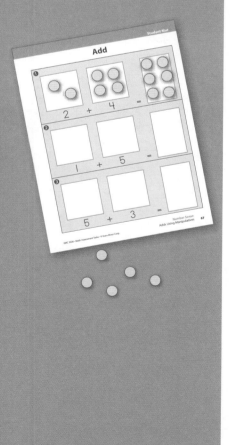

Model the Task

Place 10 counters (or beans) in a pile on the table. Say:

> Today you will use these counters to add. I will show you what to do.

Place the **teacher mat** in front of the student. Place the counters in the boxes as you say:

> Look at the number sentence. I put 3 counters here and 2 counters here. Now I count. 1, 2, 3, 4, 5. I put 5 counters in the big box. I can read the number sentence—3 plus 2 equals 5.

Student Task

Place the **student mat** in front of the student. Cover all the rows except row 1 with a blank sheet of paper. Say:

> Let's begin. Put the counters in the boxes.

Indicate the two boxes where the student places the counters. Student places 2 counters and 4 counters in the boxes. Then say:

> Count the counters. Put that many counters in the big box. Then read the number sentence.

Student responds. The class checklist is divided into two sections. Record the student's counting ability in the section labeled **Counts.** Record the student's adding ability in the section labeled **Adds.**

Clear the mat. Repeat the procedure and the script modeled above for rows 2 and 3.

Add

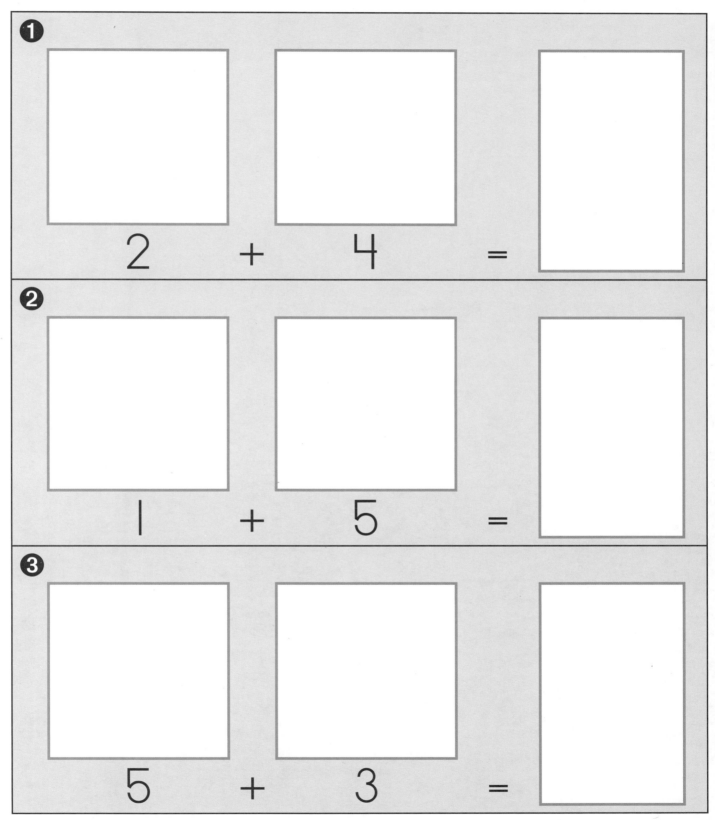

1 2 + 4 =

2 1 + 5 =

3 5 + 3 =

Number Sense
Adds Using Manipulatives **67**

Adds Using Manipulatives

Number Sense

EMC 3026 • © Evan-Moor Corp.

Add

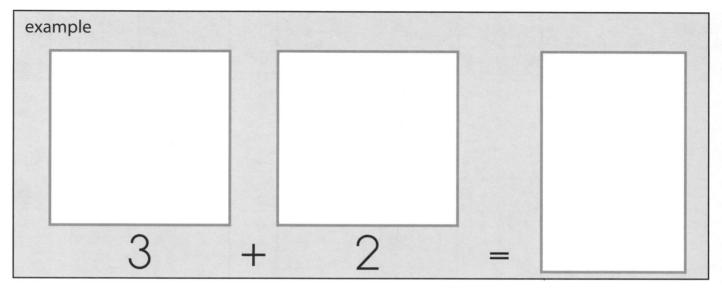

example

3 + 2 =

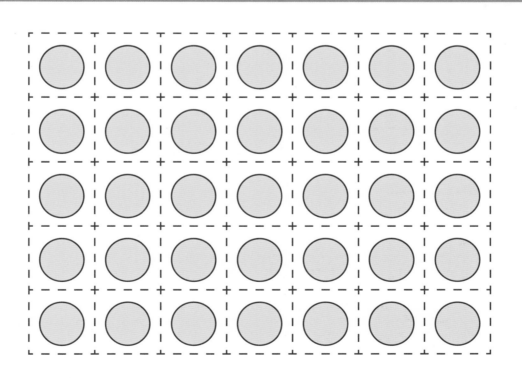

Number Sense
Adds Using Manipulatives **69**

Adds Using Manipulatives

Number Sense

EMC 3026 • © Evan-Moor Corp.

Adds Using Manipulatives	Adds Using Manipulatives	Adds Using Manipulatives	Adds Using Manipulatives	Adds Using Manipulatives	Adds Using Manipulatives	Adds Using Manipulatives
Number Sense	Number Sense	Number Sense	Number Sense	Number Sense	Number Sense	Number Sense
EMC 3026 © Evan-Moor Corp.	EMC 3026 © Evan-Moor Corp.	EMC 3026 © Evan-Moor Corp.	EMC 3026 © Evan-Moor Corp.	EMC 3026 © Evan-Moor Corp.	EMC 3026 © Evan-Moor Corp.	EMC 3026 © Evan-Moor Corp.
Adds Using Manipulatives	Adds Using Manipulatives	Adds Using Manipulatives	Adds Using Manipulatives	Adds Using Manipulatives	Adds Using Manipulatives	Adds Using Manipulatives
Number Sense	Number Sense	Number Sense	Number Sense	Number Sense	Number Sense	Number Sense
EMC 3026 © Evan-Moor Corp.	EMC 3026 © Evan-Moor Corp.	EMC 3026 © Evan-Moor Corp.	EMC 3026 © Evan-Moor Corp.	EMC 3026 © Evan-Moor Corp.	EMC 3026 © Evan-Moor Corp.	EMC 3026 © Evan-Moor Corp.
Adds Using Manipulatives	Adds Using Manipulatives	Adds Using Manipulatives	Adds Using Manipulatives	Adds Using Manipulatives	Adds Using Manipulatives	Adds Using Manipulatives
Number Sense	Number Sense	Number Sense	Number Sense	Number Sense	Number Sense	Number Sense
EMC 3026 © Evan-Moor Corp.	EMC 3026 © Evan-Moor Corp.	EMC 3026 © Evan-Moor Corp.	EMC 3026 © Evan-Moor Corp.	EMC 3026 © Evan-Moor Corp.	EMC 3026 © Evan-Moor Corp.	EMC 3026 © Evan-Moor Corp.
Adds Using Manipulatives	Adds Using Manipulatives	Adds Using Manipulatives	Adds Using Manipulatives	Adds Using Manipulatives	Adds Using Manipulatives	Adds Using Manipulatives
Number Sense	Number Sense	Number Sense	Number Sense	Number Sense	Number Sense	Number Sense
EMC 3026 © Evan-Moor Corp.	EMC 3026 © Evan-Moor Corp.	EMC 3026 © Evan-Moor Corp.	EMC 3026 © Evan-Moor Corp.	EMC 3026 © Evan-Moor Corp.	EMC 3026 © Evan-Moor Corp.	EMC 3026 © Evan-Moor Corp.
Adds Using Manipulatives	Adds Using Manipulatives	Adds Using Manipulatives	Adds Using Manipulatives	Adds Using Manipulatives	Adds Using Manipulatives	Adds Using Manipulatives
Number Sense	Number Sense	Number Sense	Number Sense	Number Sense	Number Sense	Number Sense
EMC 3026 © Evan-Moor Corp.	EMC 3026 © Evan-Moor Corp.	EMC 3026 © Evan-Moor Corp.	EMC 3026 © Evan-Moor Corp.	EMC 3026 © Evan-Moor Corp.	EMC 3026 © Evan-Moor Corp.	EMC 3026 © Evan-Moor Corp.

Adds Using Manipulatives

Class Checklist		Key: **+** correct response **−** incorrect response ● self-corrected						
Name	**Date**	**Counts**			**Adds**			**Notes**
		6	6	8	2+4=6	1+5=6	5+3=8	

Name _____

I Can Add

Cut out and glue the apples. Use them to add.

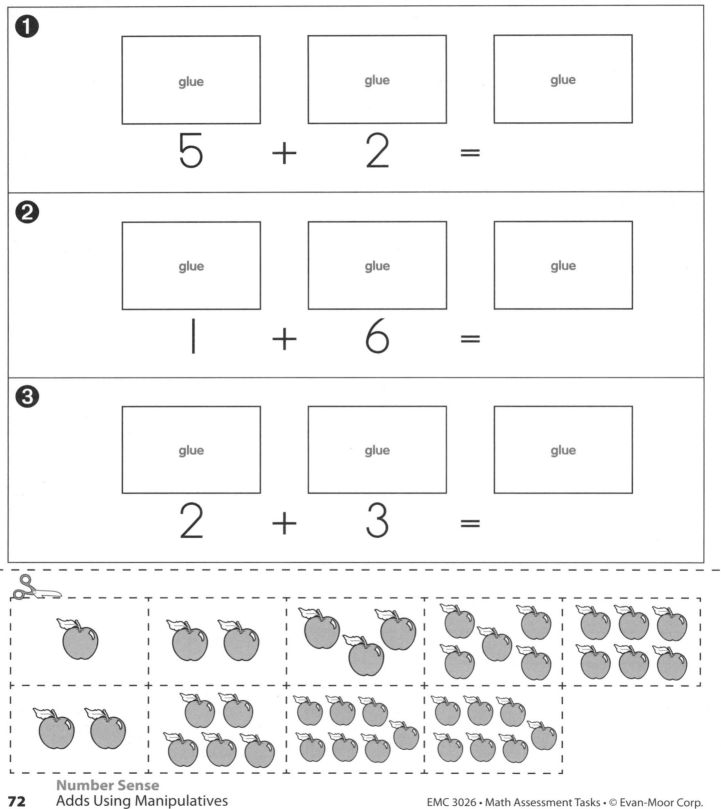

❶

| glue | glue | glue |

$$5 \quad + \quad 2 \quad =$$

❷

| glue | glue | glue |

$$1 \quad + \quad 6 \quad =$$

❸

| glue | glue | glue |

$$2 \quad + \quad 3 \quad =$$

Subtracts Using Manipulatives

Objective:
Student uses concrete objects to subtract one-digit numbers.

Materials:
Mat, p. 75

Counters, p. 77
(or you may use beans)

Class Checklist, p. 79

Activity Sheet, p. 80

Blank sheet of paper

Model the Task

Place 10 counters (or beans) in a pile on the table. Say:

> Today you will use these counters to subtract. I will show you what to do.

Place the mat in front of the student. Cover all the rows with a blank sheet of paper except for the example. Place 4 counters in the box as you say:

> Look at the number sentence. I put 4 counters in the box. I need to take 1 away.

Remove 1 counter.

> Now I count what's left. 1, 2, 3. I can read the number sentence — 4 minus 1 equals 3.

Student Task

Clear the mat. Move the paper down the mat to reveal row 1. Say:

> Let's begin. Put the counters in the box.

Student places 5 counters in the box. Say:

> How many counters do you need to take away?

Student removes 2 counters. Say:

> How many counters are left?

Student responds. Record student's response on the class checklist.

Repeat the procedure and the script modeled above for rows 2 and 3.

Subtract

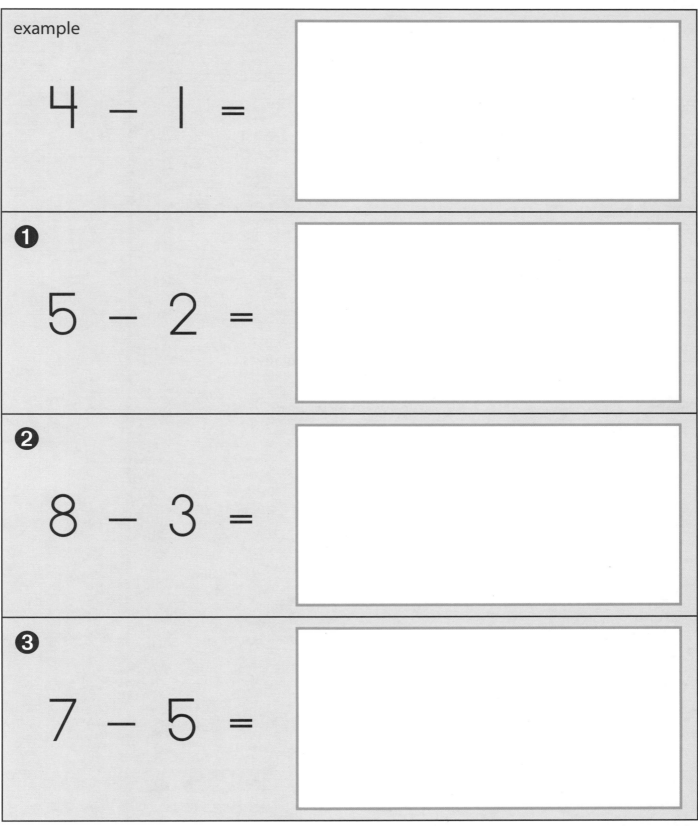

example

$4 - 1 =$

1 $5 - 2 =$

2 $8 - 3 =$

3 $7 - 5 =$

Subtracts Using Manipulatives

Number Sense

EMC 3026 • © Evan-Moor Corp.

Number Sense
Subtracts Using Manipulatives   **77**

Subtracts Using Manipulatives Number Sense EMC 3026 © Evan-Moor Corp.	**Subtracts Using Manipulatives** Number Sense EMC 3026 © Evan-Moor Corp.	**Subtracts Using Manipulatives** Number Sense EMC 3026 © Evan-Moor Corp.	**Subtracts Using Manipulatives** Number Sense EMC 3026 © Evan-Moor Corp.	**Subtracts Using Manipulatives** Number Sense EMC 3026 © Evan-Moor Corp.	**Subtracts Using Manipulatives** Number Sense EMC 3026 © Evan-Moor Corp.	**Subtracts Using Manipulatives** Number Sense EMC 3026 © Evan-Moor Corp.
Subtracts Using Manipulatives Number Sense EMC 3026 © Evan-Moor Corp.	**Subtracts Using Manipulatives** Number Sense EMC 3026 © Evan-Moor Corp.	**Subtracts Using Manipulatives** Number Sense EMC 3026 © Evan-Moor Corp.	**Subtracts Using Manipulatives** Number Sense EMC 3026 © Evan-Moor Corp.	**Subtracts Using Manipulatives** Number Sense EMC 3026 © Evan-Moor Corp.	**Subtracts Using Manipulatives** Number Sense EMC 3026 © Evan-Moor Corp.	**Subtracts Using Manipulatives** Number Sense EMC 3026 © Evan-Moor Corp.
Subtracts Using Manipulatives Number Sense EMC 3026 © Evan-Moor Corp.	**Subtracts Using Manipulatives** Number Sense EMC 3026 © Evan-Moor Corp.	**Subtracts Using Manipulatives** Number Sense EMC 3026 © Evan-Moor Corp.	**Subtracts Using Manipulatives** Number Sense EMC 3026 © Evan-Moor Corp.	**Subtracts Using Manipulatives** Number Sense EMC 3026 © Evan-Moor Corp.	**Subtracts Using Manipulatives** Number Sense EMC 3026 © Evan-Moor Corp.	**Subtracts Using Manipulatives** Number Sense EMC 3026 © Evan-Moor Corp.
Subtracts Using Manipulatives Number Sense EMC 3026 © Evan-Moor Corp.	**Subtracts Using Manipulatives** Number Sense EMC 3026 © Evan-Moor Corp.	**Subtracts Using Manipulatives** Number Sense EMC 3026 © Evan-Moor Corp.	**Subtracts Using Manipulatives** Number Sense EMC 3026 © Evan-Moor Corp.	**Subtracts Using Manipulatives** Number Sense EMC 3026 © Evan-Moor Corp.	**Subtracts Using Manipulatives** Number Sense EMC 3026 © Evan-Moor Corp.	**Subtracts Using Manipulatives** Number Sense EMC 3026 © Evan-Moor Corp.
Subtracts Using Manipulatives Number Sense EMC 3026 © Evan-Moor Corp.	**Subtracts Using Manipulatives** Number Sense EMC 3026 © Evan-Moor Corp.	**Subtracts Using Manipulatives** Number Sense EMC 3026 © Evan-Moor Corp.	**Subtracts Using Manipulatives** Number Sense EMC 3026 © Evan-Moor Corp.	**Subtracts Using Manipulatives** Number Sense EMC 3026 © Evan-Moor Corp.	**Subtracts Using Manipulatives** Number Sense EMC 3026 © Evan-Moor Corp.	**Subtracts Using Manipulatives** Number Sense EMC 3026 © Evan-Moor Corp.

Subtracts Using Manipulatives

Class Checklist		Key: + correct response − incorrect response ● self-corrected				
Name	Date	**Row 1** 5 − 2 = 3	**2** 8 − 3 = 5	**3** 7 − 5 = 2	Notes	

Note: Student subtracts using pictures.

Name _____

Take Away

Cross out. Write how many are left.

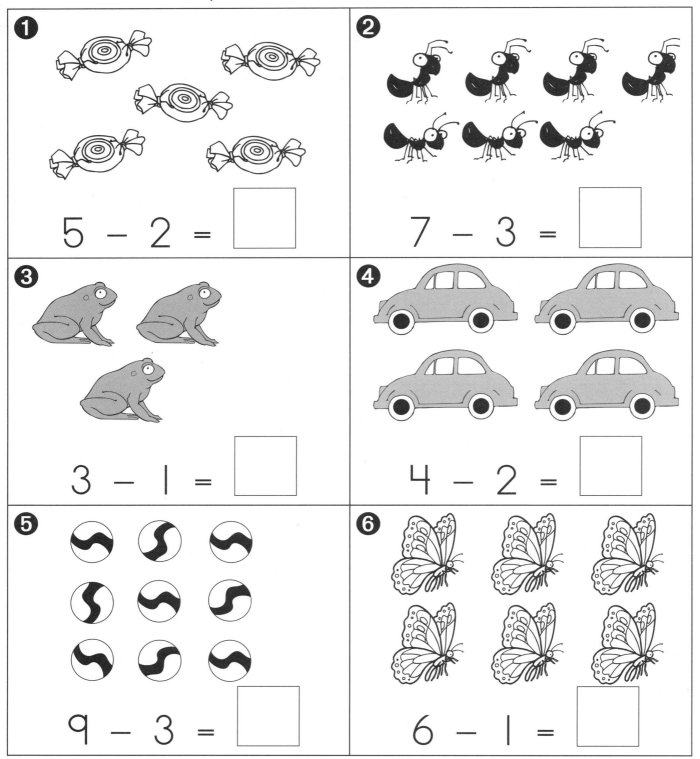

1

$5 - 2 =$ ☐

2

$7 - 3 =$ ☐

3

$3 - 1 =$ ☐

4

$4 - 2 =$ ☐

5

$9 - 3 =$ ☐

6

$6 - 1 =$ ☐

Objective:
Student makes reasonable estimates regarding how many objects are in a pictured container.

Materials:
Number Cards, p. 83

Class Checklist, p. 85

Activity Sheet, p. 86

Student Task

Say:

> Today you will look at pictures. You will guess how many things are in each picture.

Hold the cards in order from 1 to 4. Show card 1 to the student. Say:

> Let's begin. About how many balls are in the box — 5 or 50?

Student responds. Record the response on the class checklist. Show card 2 and say:

> About how many balls are in the box — 3 or 30?

Record the response. Show card 3 and say:

> About how many balls are in the box — 2 or 20?

Record the response. Show card 4 and say:

> About how many balls are in the box — 4 or 40?

Record the response.

Makes Reasonable Estimates

| Class Checklist | Key: | + correct response | − incorrect response | ● self-corrected |

Makes Reasonable Estimates

Class Checklist — Key: **+** correct response **−** incorrect response **●** self-corrected

Name	Date	Card 1 5	2 30	3 20	4 4	Notes

Name _____

Activity Sheet

Let Me Guess

Circle the correct answer.

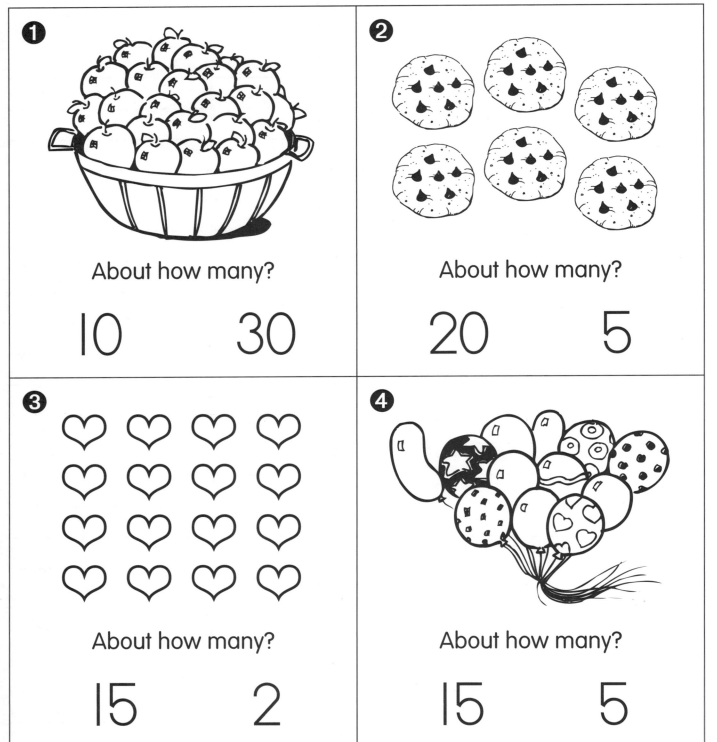

❶ About how many?

10   30

❷ About how many?

20   5

❸ About how many?

15   2

❹ About how many?

15   5

Unit 2
Measurement and Geometry

Quick Checks

Student Task

Say:

> Today you will show what is short and what is long.

Arrange the picture cards in random order on the table. Place the mat in front of the student. Point to box 1 on the mat. Say:

> Let's begin. Put the shortest carrot here. Then put the next shortest. Keep going until you end with the longest carrot.

Student responds. Record the response on the class checklist.

Objective:
Student compares the length of pictured objects by arranging them in order from shortest to longest.

Materials:
Mat, p. 91
Picture Cards, p. 93
Class Checklist, p. 95
Activity Sheet, p. 96

Short and Long

Short and Long

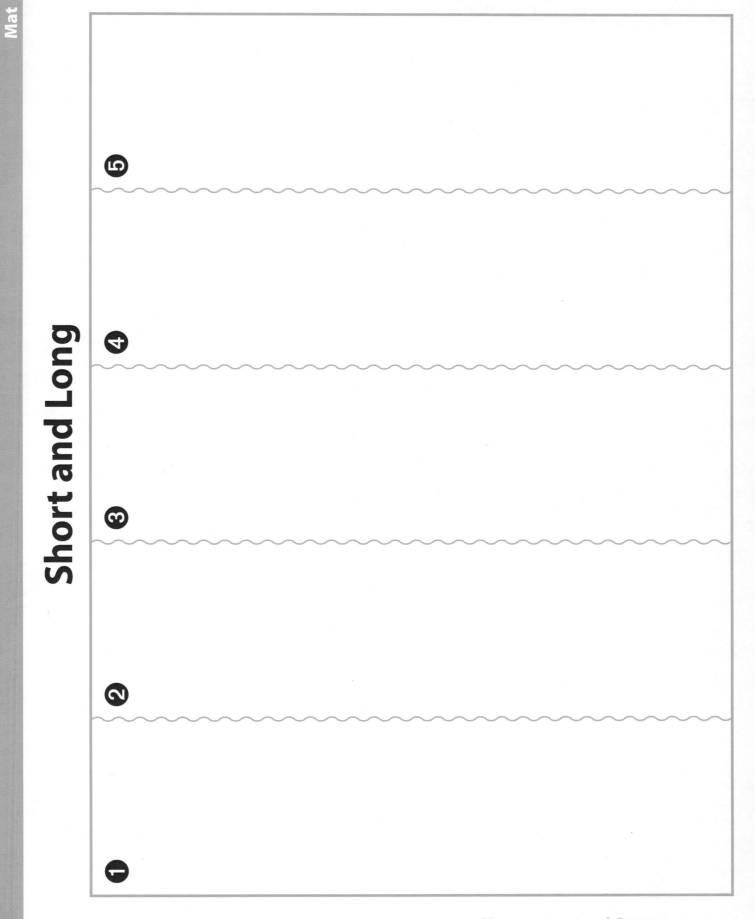

Compares Objects by Length

Measurement and Geometry

EMC 3026 • © Evan-Moor Corp.

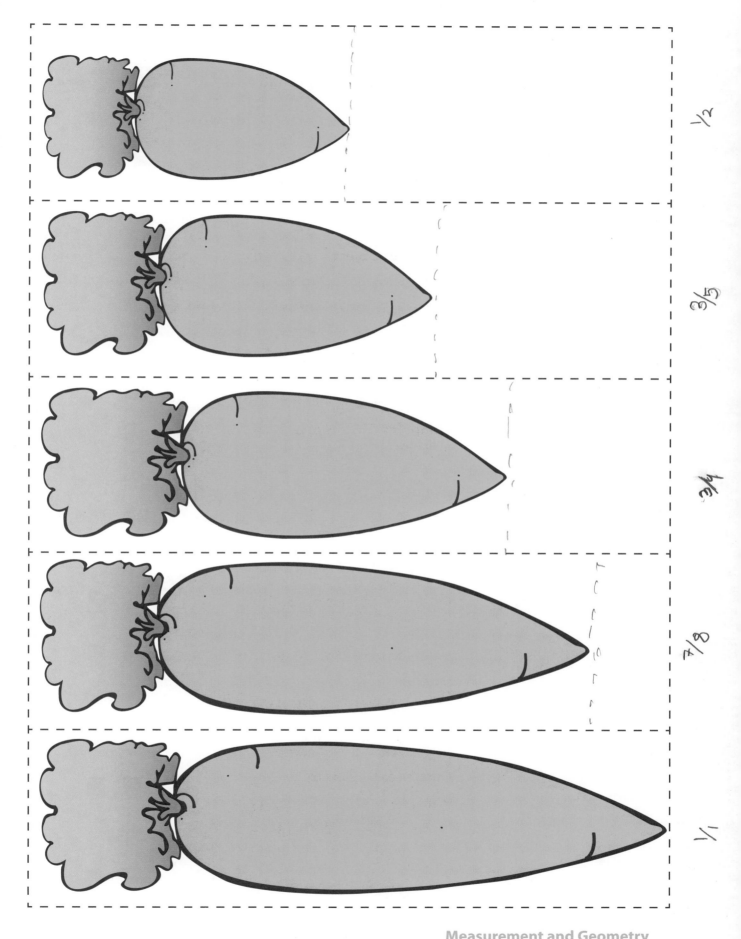

½

⅗

¾

⅞

1/1

Compares Objects by Length

Measurement and Geometry

EMC 3026 • © Evan-Moor Corp.

Compares Objects by Length

Measurement and Geometry

EMC 3026 • © Evan-Moor Corp.

Compares Objects by Length

Measurement and Geometry

EMC 3026 • © Evan-Moor Corp.

Compares Objects by Length

Measurement and Geometry

EMC 3026 • © Evan-Moor Corp.

Compares Objects by Length

Measurement and Geometry

EMC 3026 • © Evan-Moor Corp.

Compares Objects by Length

Class Checklist	Key:	+ correct response	– incorrect response	● self-corrected

Name	Date	Shortest to Longest	Notes

Name _____

Take a Good Look

Circle the correct answer.

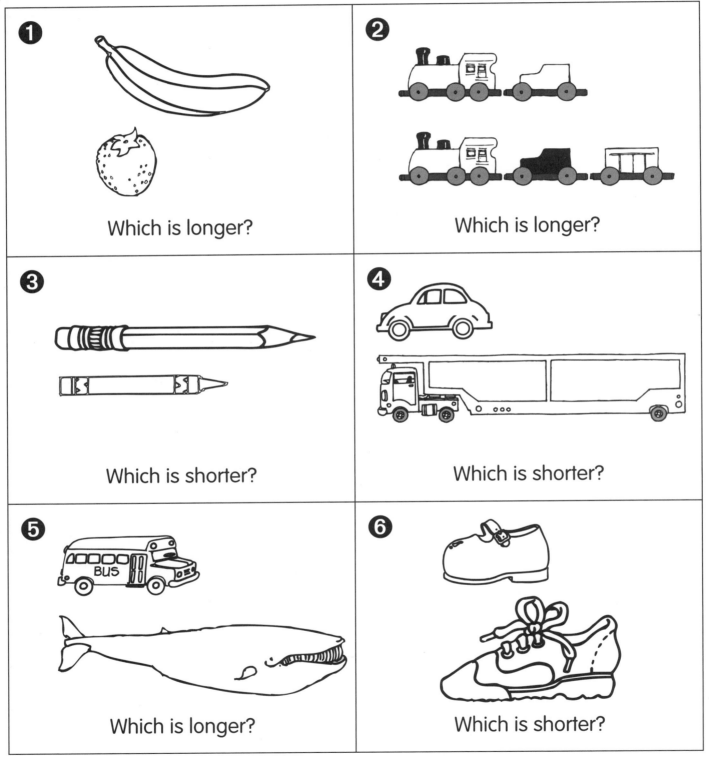

1 Which is longer?

2 Which is longer?

3 Which is shorter?

4 Which is shorter?

5 Which is longer?

6 Which is shorter?

Compares Objects by Weight

Model the Task

Say:

> Today you will show what is heavy and what is light. I will show you what to do.

Place the mat in front of the student. Place the wagon cards as you say:

> Look at the seesaw. Things that are heavy push the end down. A wagon with toys is heavier than an empty wagon. The wagon with toys goes here. The empty wagon goes on the end that is up.

Student Task

Show the truck cards and say:

> Let's begin. Put the trucks on the seesaw.

Student responds. Record the student's response on the class checklist. Then show the bike cards and say:

> Put the bikes on the seesaw.

Record the response. Show the car cards and say:

> Put the cars on the seesaw.

Record the response.

Objective:
Student compares the weight of pictured objects as heavier or lighter.

Materials:
Mat, p. 99

Picture Cards, p. 101

Class Checklist, p. 103

Activity Sheet, p. 104

Light and Heavy

example

example

Light and Heavy

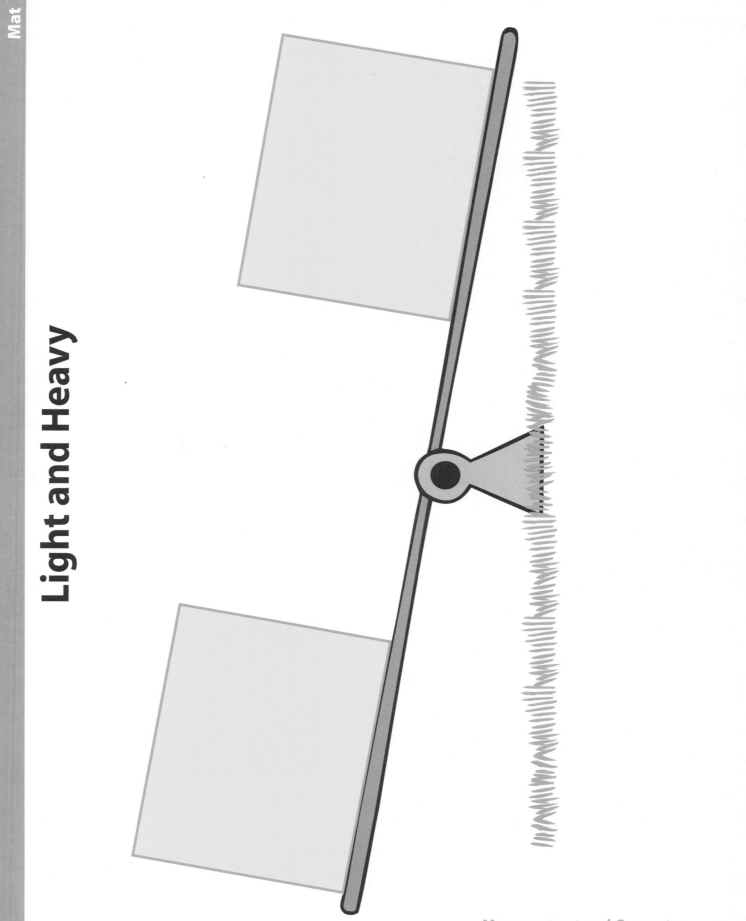

Measurement and Geometry
Compares Objects by Weight **99**

example

example

①

①

②

②

③

③

EMC 3026 • Math Assessment Tasks • © Evan-Moor Corp.

Compares Objects by Weight

Measurement and Geometry

EMC 3026 • © Evan-Moor Corp.

Compares Objects by Weight

Measurement and Geometry

EMC 3026 • © Evan-Moor Corp.

Compares Objects by Weight

Measurement and Geometry

EMC 3026 • © Evan-Moor Corp.

Compares Objects by Weight

Measurement and Geometry

EMC 3026 • © Evan-Moor Corp.

Compares Objects by Weight

Measurement and Geometry

EMC 3026 • © Evan-Moor Corp.

Compares Objects by Weight

Measurement and Geometry

EMC 3026 • © Evan-Moor Corp.

Compares Objects by Weight

Measurement and Geometry

EMC 3026 • © Evan-Moor Corp.

Compares Objects by Weight

Measurement and Geometry

EMC 3026 • © Evan-Moor Corp.

Compares Objects by Weight

Class Checklist					
Key:		**+** correct response	**−** incorrect response	**●** self-corrected	

Name	Date	Trucks	Bikes	Cars	Notes

Name _____

Seesaw

Look at each seesaw. Circle the heavier animal.
Make an **X** on the lighter animal.

Measurement and Geometry
Compares Objects by Capacity

Objective:
Student compares the capacity of pictured containers as to which holds more.

Materials:
Mat, p. 107

Picture Cards, p. 109

Class Checklist, p. 111

Activity Sheet, p. 112

Model the Task

Say:

> Today you will look at pictures and show which object holds more. I will show you what to do.

Place the mat in front of the student. Show the two examples and place the van on the mat as you say:

> Look at the two cars. A van holds *more* than a small car. I will put the van card on the mat.

Student Task

Show the two glass cards and say:

> Let's begin. Put the glass that holds *more* on the mat.

Student responds. Record the response on the class checklist. Show the two bag cards and say:

> Put the bag that holds *more* on the mat.

Record the response. Show the two pot cards and say:

> Put the pot that holds *more* on the mat.

Record the response.

EMC 3026 • Math Assessment Tasks • © Evan-Moor Corp.

Holds More

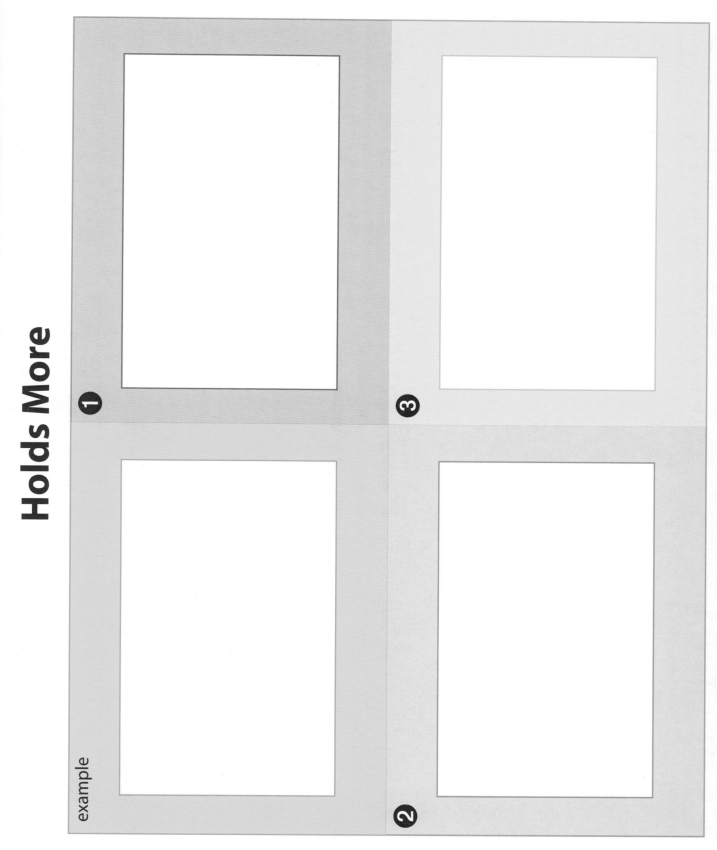

example

❶

❸

❷

Measurement and Geometry
Compares Objects by Capacity   **107**

Compares Objects by Capacity

Measurement and Geometry

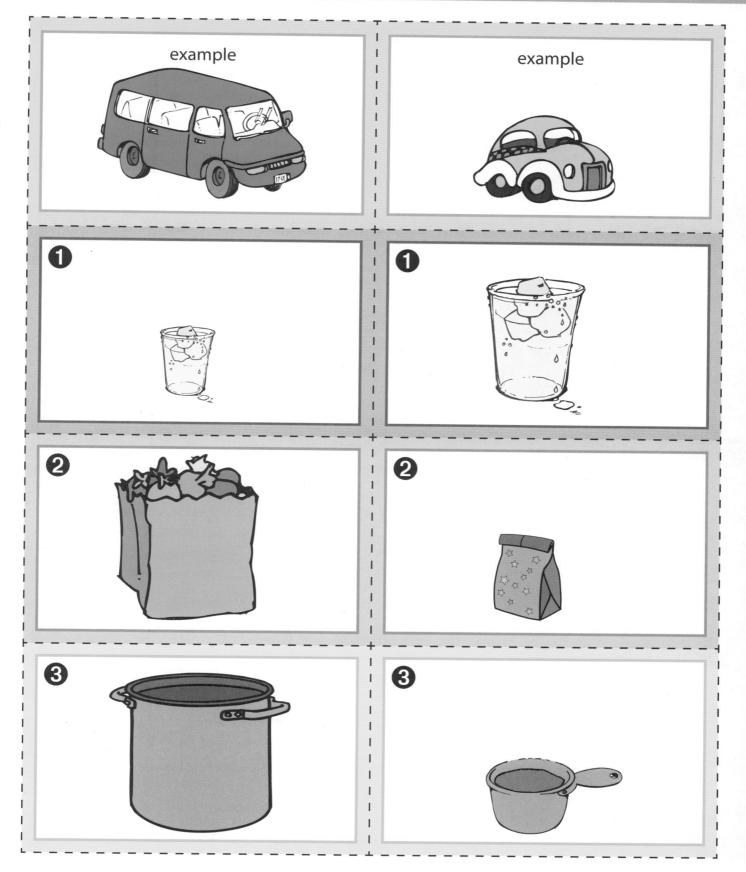

example

example

❶

❶

❷

❷

❸

❸

Measurement and Geometry
Compares Objects by Capacity **109**

Compares Objects by Capacity
Measurement and Geometry
EMC 3026 • © Evan-Moor Corp.

Compares Objects by Capacity
Measurement and Geometry
EMC 3026 • © Evan-Moor Corp.

Compares Objects by Capacity
Measurement and Geometry
EMC 3026 • © Evan-Moor Corp.

Compares Objects by Capacity
Measurement and Geometry
EMC 3026 • © Evan-Moor Corp.

Compares Objects by Capacity
Measurement and Geometry
EMC 3026 • © Evan-Moor Corp.

Compares Objects by Capacity
Measurement and Geometry
EMC 3026 • © Evan-Moor Corp.

Compares Objects by Capacity
Measurement and Geometry
EMC 3026 • © Evan-Moor Corp.

Compares Objects by Capacity
Measurement and Geometry
EMC 3026 • © Evan-Moor Corp.

Compares Objects by Capacity

Class Checklist		Key: + correct response − incorrect response • self-corrected				
Name	Date	**Card 1** Large Glass	**2** Grocery Bag	**3** Large Pot		Notes

Name _____

Holders

Color what holds more.
Make an **X** on what holds less.

Objective:
Student names the days of the week in order.

Materials:
Puzzle Pieces, p. 115

Class Checklist, p. 117

Activity Sheet, p. 118

Model the Task

Say:

> Today you will make a puzzle about the days of the week. I will show you what to do.

Place the puzzle pieces on the table in random order. Take the puzzle piece labeled **Sunday** and say:

> Let's begin. Sunday is the first day of the week. Now you say the next day. I will give you the piece to fit.

Student names the day. Hand the student the corresponding puzzle piece. (If you have students who can read the names of the days of the week, they may find the puzzle pieces on their own.)

Then say:

> What day comes next?

Student responds. Hand the student the corresponding puzzle piece.

Repeat the procedure and the script modeled above until the student names all of the days. Use the completed puzzle as a reference to record the student's responses on the class checklist.

Days of the Week

Sunday

Monday

Tuesday

Wednesday

Thursday

Friday

Saturday

Measurement and Geometry
Names the Days of the Week **115**

Names the Days of the Week

Measurement and Geometry

EMC 3026 • © Evan-Moor Corp.

Names the Days of the Week

Measurement and Geometry

EMC 3026 • © Evan-Moor Corp.

Names the Days of the Week

Measurement and Geometry

EMC 3026 • © Evan-Moor Corp.

Names the Days of the Week

Measurement and Geometry

EMC 3026 • © Evan-Moor Corp.

Names the Days of the Week

Measurement and Geometry

EMC 3026 • © Evan-Moor Corp.

Names the Days of the Week

Measurement and Geometry

EMC 3026 • © Evan-Moor Corp.

Names the Days of the Week

Measurement and Geometry

EMC 3026 • © Evan-Moor Corp.

Names the Days of the Week

Class Checklist		Key: + correct response − incorrect response ● self-corrected	
Name	Date	Names the Days of the Week in Order	Notes

Name _____

A Fun Day

Tell someone the days of the week.
Draw what you like to do on Saturday.

Hooray for Me!
I can say the days of the week.

Quick Checks

Objective:
Student identifies the time when everyday events occur.

Materials:
Puzzle Pieces, pp. 121 and 123

Class Checklist, p. 125

Activity Sheet, p. 126

Student Task

Say:

> Today you will make a puzzle about time.

Hold the three clock puzzle pieces. Place the six picture puzzle pieces faceup in random order on the table. Show clock 1 to the student. Say:

> Let's begin. This is 7 o'clock in the morning. Fit together two puzzle pieces that show what you can do at 7 o'clock in the morning.

Student responds. Record the response on the class checklist. Then show clock 2. Say:

> This is 12 o'clock in the afternoon. Fit together two puzzle pieces that show what you can do at 12 o'clock in the afternoon.

Record the response. Then show clock 3. Say:

> This is 8 o'clock at night. Fit together two puzzle pieces that show what you can do at 8 o'clock at night.

Record the response.

Telling Time

1 7:00 a.m.

2 12:00 p.m.

3 8:00 p.m.

Measurement and Geometry
Identifies the Time of Events

Identifies the Time of Events

Measurement and Geometry

EMC 3026 • © Evan-Moor Corp.

Identifies the Time of Events

Measurement and Geometry

EMC 3026 • © Evan-Moor Corp.

Identifies the Time of Events

Measurement and Geometry

EMC 3026 • © Evan-Moor Corp.

Identifies the Time of Events

Measurement and Geometry

EMC 3026 • © Evan-Moor Corp.

Identifies the Time of Events

Measurement and Geometry

EMC 3026 • © Evan-Moor Corp.

Identifies the Time of Events

Measurement and Geometry

EMC 3026 • © Evan-Moor Corp.

Telling Time

Measurement and Geometry
Identifies the Time of Events **123**

Identifies the Time of Events

Measurement and Geometry

EMC 3026 • © Evan-Moor Corp.

Identifies the Time of Events

Measurement and Geometry

EMC 3026 • © Evan-Moor Corp.

Identifies the Time of Events

Measurement and Geometry

EMC 3026 • © Evan-Moor Corp.

Identifies the Time of Events

Class Checklist

Key: **+** correct response **–** incorrect response ● self-corrected
Puzzle pieces are color-coded on the back for checking.

Name	Date	**Morning**	**Afternoon**	**Night**	Notes

Name _____

My Day

Draw something you do at each time.

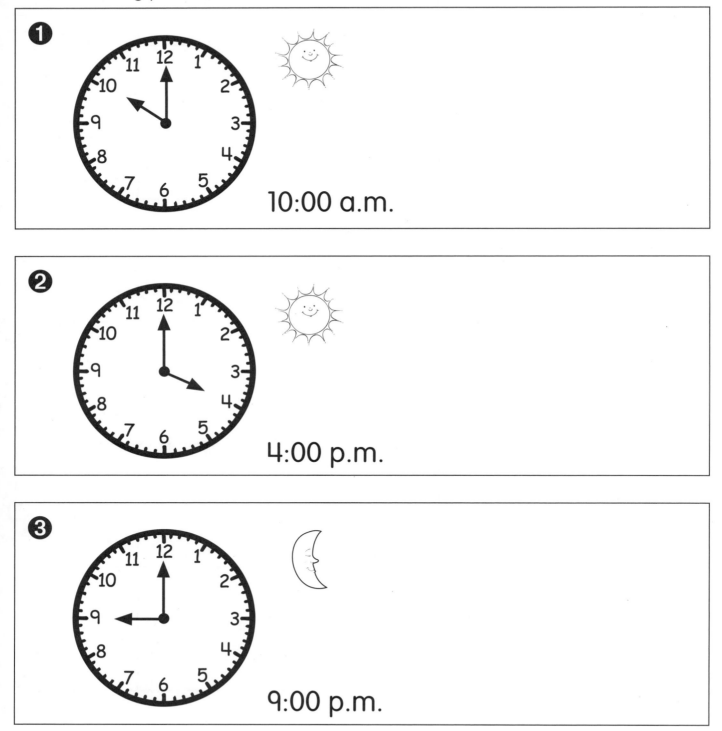

1

10:00 a.m.

2

4:00 p.m.

3

9:00 p.m.

Names and Identifies Plane Shapes

Objective:
Student names and identifies four common plane shapes.

Materials:
Mat, p. 129
Shape Cards, p. 131
Class Checklist, p. 133
Activity Sheet, p. 134

Student Task

Say:

> Today you will tell me about shapes.

Show the shape cards one at a time. As you show each, say:

> What is the name of this shape?

Record each response on the class checklist in the section labeled **Names Shape.**

Then place the mat in front of the student. Say:

> How many circles are in the picture?

Student may point to the shapes while counting them. Record the response in the section labeled **Identifies Shape.**

Ask the following questions and pause after each to record the response:

> How many squares are in the picture?
> How many rectangles are in the picture?
> How many triangles are in the picture?

Shapes

Fred's Fruit

Measurement and Geometry
Names and Identifies Plane Shapes **129**

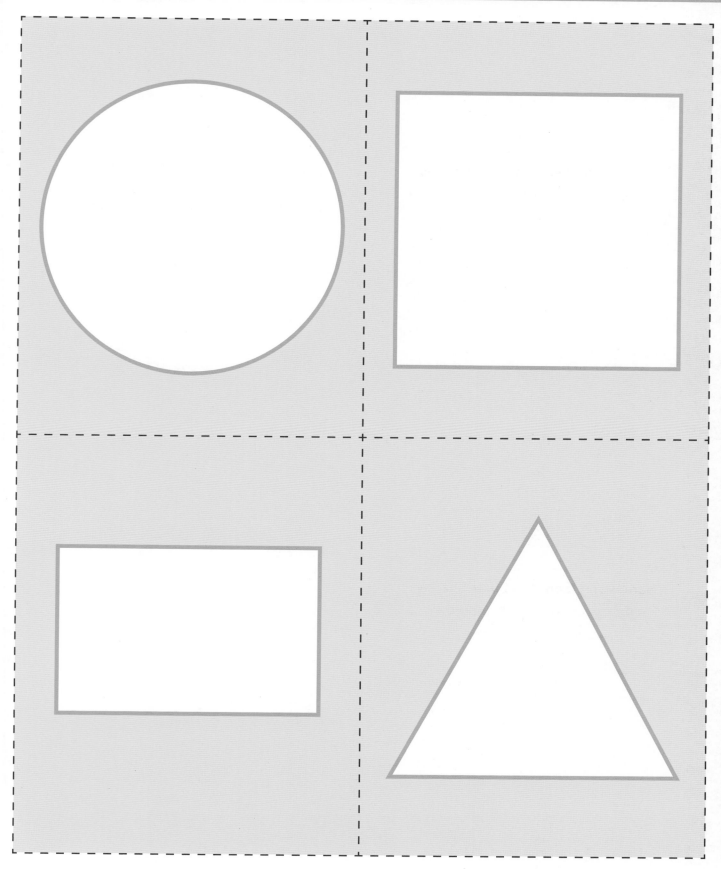

Names and Identifies Plane Shapes

Measurement and Geometry

EMC 3026 • © Evan-Moor Corp.

Names and Identifies Plane Shapes

Measurement and Geometry

EMC 3026 • © Evan-Moor Corp.

Names and Identifies Plane Shapes

Measurement and Geometry

EMC 3026 • © Evan-Moor Corp.

Names and Identifies Plane Shapes

Measurement and Geometry

EMC 3026 • © Evan-Moor Corp.

Names and Identifies Plane Shapes

Class Checklist		Key: + correct response − incorrect response ● self-corrected								
Name	**Date**	**Names Shape**				**Identifies Shape**				**Notes**
		○	□	▭	△	4○	4□	3▭	1△	

Name _____

Shape Train

Color the shapes. Color the train car.

◯ = red   ☐ = blue   △ = yellow   ▭ = green

Compares Plane and Solid Shapes

Objective:

Student identifies the plane shapes that form part of familiar solid objects.

Materials:

Mat, p. 137

Shape Cards, p. 139

Class Checklist, p. 141

Activity Sheet, p. 142

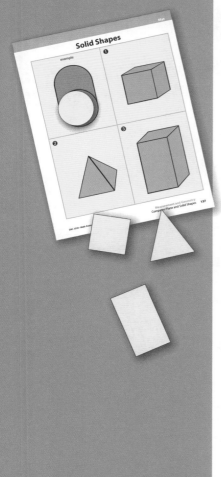

Model the Task

Say:

> Today you will look for shapes. I will show you what to do.

Place the shape cards faceup on the table. Place the mat in front of the student. Point to the example and say:

> Here is a block. Part of this block is a circle. I will put the circle card on the block.

Place the circle card on the circular end of the cylinder.

Student Task

Point to box 1 and say:

> Let's begin. Look at the block. One side has a shape. Put that shape on the block.

Student responds. Record the response on the class checklist. Then point to box 2 and say:

> Look at the block. One side has a shape. Put that shape on the block.

Record the response. Point to box 3 and say:

> Look at the block. One side has a shape. Put that shape on the block.

Record the response.

Solid Shapes

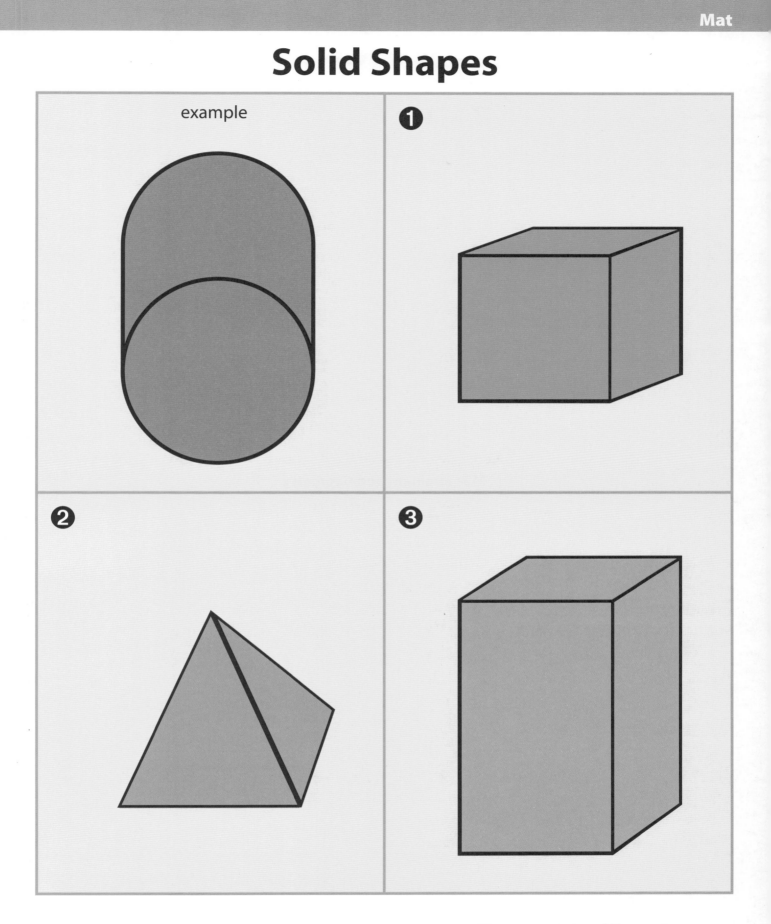

example

❶

❷

❸

Compares Plane and Solid Shapes

EMC 3026 • © Evan-Moor Corp.

Compares Plane and Solid Shapes

Name	Date	Box 1 Square	2 Triangle	3 Rectangle	Notes

Class Checklist

Key: + correct response − incorrect response ● self-corrected

Name _____

What Am I?

Circle the correct shape.

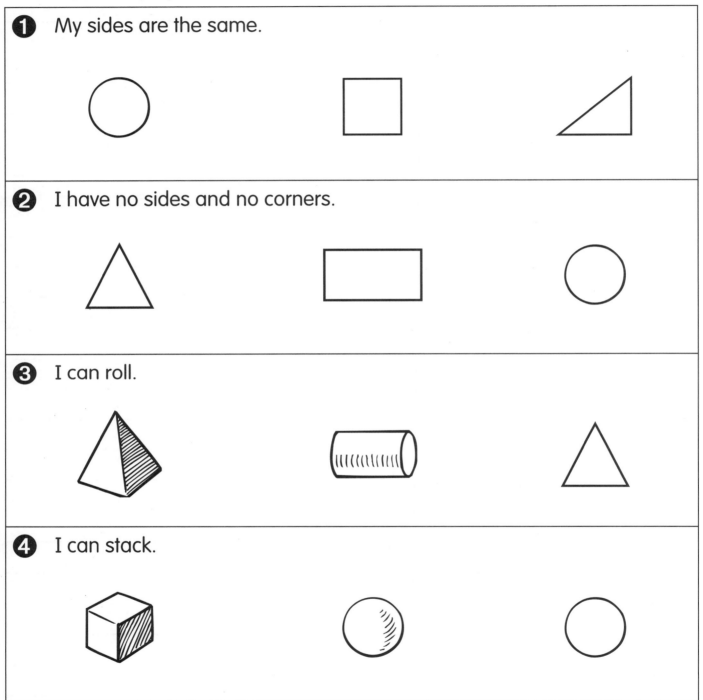

1 My sides are the same.

2 I have no sides and no corners.

3 I can roll.

4 I can stack.

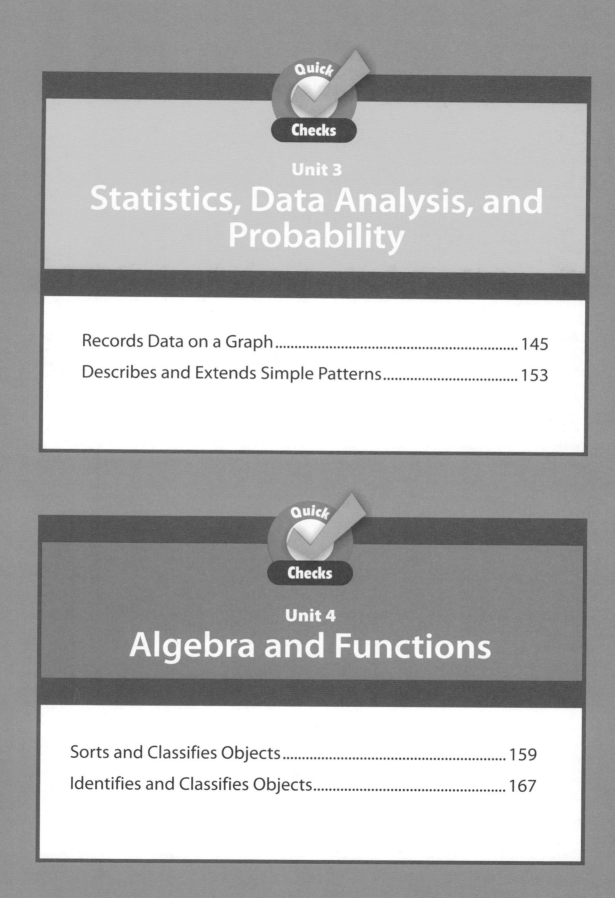

Quick Checks

Unit 3
Statistics, Data Analysis, and Probability

Quick Checks

Unit 4
Algebra and Functions

Records Data on a Graph

Objective:
Student records given data on a picture graph.

Materials:
Mat, p. 147

Pet Store List, p. 149

Picture Squares, p. 149

Class Checklist, p. 151

Activity Sheet, p. 152

Student Task

Say:

> Today you will make a picture graph.

Place the picture squares in four piles on the table. Place the mat and the pet store list in front of the student. Say:

> Let's begin. Look at the pet store list. Use the dog squares to show how many dogs are in the pet store. Put the dog squares in the correct place on the mat.

Student responds. Record the student's response on the class checklist. Then say:

> Now show how many cats are in the pet store.

Record the response.

Repeat the procedure and the script modeled above for the mice and lizards.

Picture Graph

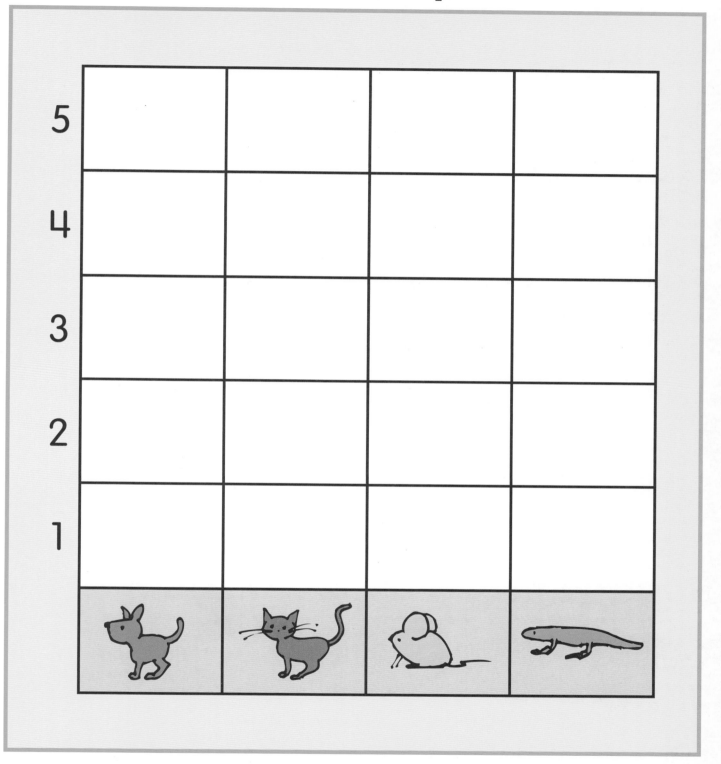

Records Data on a Graph

Statistics, Data Analysis, and Probability

EMC 3026 • © Evan-Moor Corp.

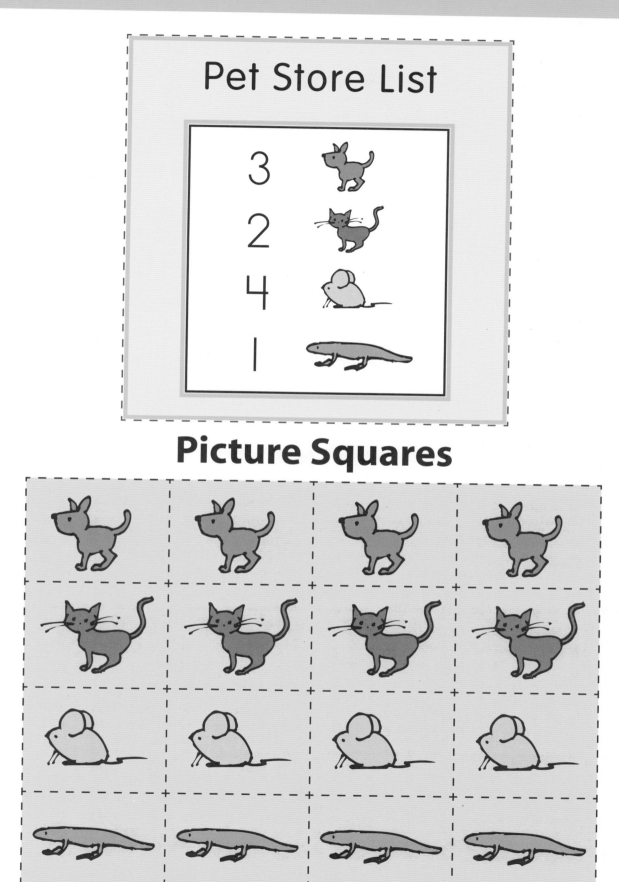

Pet Store List

Picture Squares

Statistics, Data Analysis, and Probability
Records Data on a Graph **149**

Records Data on a Graph

Statistics, Data Analysis, and Probability

EMC 3026 • © Evan-Moor Corp.

Records Data on a Graph Statistics, Data Analysis, and Probability EMC 3026 • © Evan-Moor Corp.	**Records Data on a Graph** Statistics, Data Analysis, and Probability EMC 3026 • © Evan-Moor Corp.	**Records Data on a Graph** Statistics, Data Analysis, and Probability EMC 3026 • © Evan-Moor Corp.	**Records Data on a Graph** Statistics, Data Analysis, and Probability EMC 3026 • © Evan-Moor Corp.
Records Data on a Graph Statistics, Data Analysis, and Probability EMC 3026 • © Evan-Moor Corp.	**Records Data on a Graph** Statistics, Data Analysis, and Probability EMC 3026 • © Evan-Moor Corp.	**Records Data on a Graph** Statistics, Data Analysis, and Probability EMC 3026 • © Evan-Moor Corp.	**Records Data on a Graph** Statistics, Data Analysis, and Probability EMC 3026 • © Evan-Moor Corp.
Records Data on a Graph Statistics, Data Analysis, and Probability EMC 3026 • © Evan-Moor Corp.	**Records Data on a Graph** Statistics, Data Analysis, and Probability EMC 3026 • © Evan-Moor Corp.	**Records Data on a Graph** Statistics, Data Analysis, and Probability EMC 3026 • © Evan-Moor Corp.	**Records Data on a Graph** Statistics, Data Analysis, and Probability EMC 3026 • © Evan-Moor Corp.
Records Data on a Graph Statistics, Data Analysis, and Probability EMC 3026 • © Evan-Moor Corp.	**Records Data on a Graph** Statistics, Data Analysis, and Probability EMC 3026 • © Evan-Moor Corp.	**Records Data on a Graph** Statistics, Data Analysis, and Probability EMC 3026 • © Evan-Moor Corp.	**Records Data on a Graph** Statistics, Data Analysis, and Probability EMC 3026 • © Evan-Moor Corp.

Records Data on a Graph

Class Checklist		Key: + correct response − incorrect response ● self-corrected					
Name	Date	Dogs	Cats	Mice	Lizards	Notes	
		3 squares	2 squares	4 squares	1 square		

Name _____

Favorite Fruit

Color each row.
Show how the kids voted.

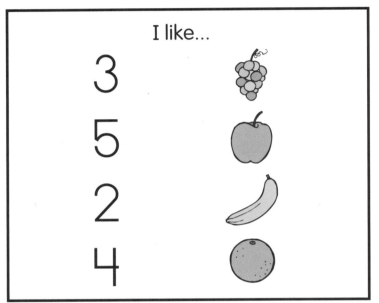

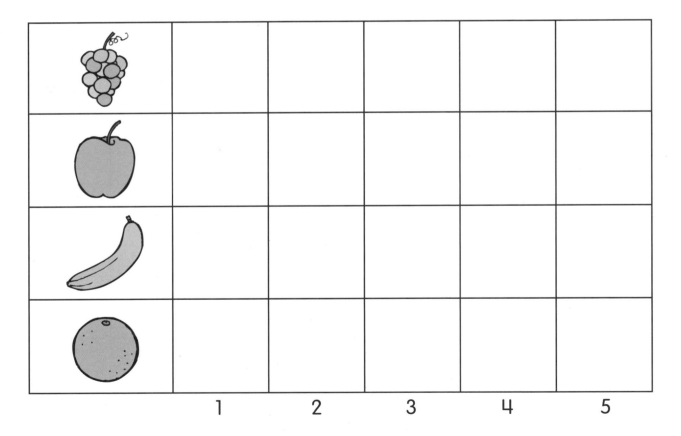

Describes and Extends Simple Patterns

Objective:

Student describes and extends given patterns.

Materials:

Mat, p. 155

Bead Cards, p. 155

Class Checklist, p. 157

Activity Sheet, p. 158

Student Task

(Note: You may adjust this task to suit the abilities of your students.)

Say:

> Today you will work with picture patterns.

Place the mat in front of the student. Arrange the bead cards in piles according to color. Point to row 1 on the mat and say:

> Let's begin. Look at the pattern in row 1. Put the beads that come next.

Student responds. Record the response on the class checklist. Use the section labeled **Extends.** Then say:

> Tell me the pattern.

Student may respond with Red Red Blue Red Red Blue or AAB AAB or 1,1,2 1,1,2. Record the response. Use the section labeled **Describes**.

Repeat the procedure and the script modeled above for row 2. Not all picture cards will be used. The pattern in row 2 may be stated as Purple Green Pink Purple Green Pink or ABC ABC or 1,2,3 1,2,3.

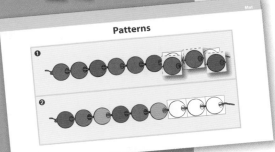

EMC 3026 • Math Assessment Tasks • © Evan-Moor Corp.

Patterns

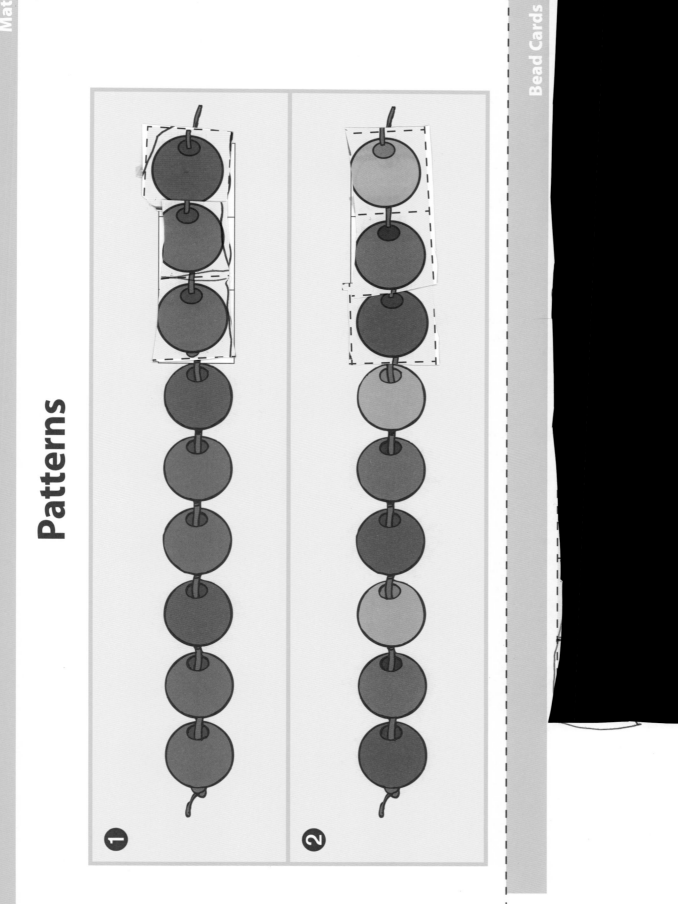

1

2

Describes and Extends Simple Patterns

Class Checklist						
Key: + correct response − incorrect response ● self-corrected						

Name	Date	Extends		Describes		Notes
		Row 1	Row 2	Row 1	Row 2	

Note: Student extends patterns.

Name _____

What Comes Next?

Finish the patterns.

EMC 3026 • Math Assessment Tasks • © Evan-Moor Corp.

Sorts and Classifies Objects

Objective:

Student sorts pictured objects into two categories and explains their classification.

Materials:

Mat, p. 161

Picture Cards, p. 163

Class Checklist, p. 165

Activity Sheet, p. 166

Student Task

Say:

> Today you will sort pictures into groups.

Place the mat in front of the student. Arrange the picture cards faceup in random order on the table. Say.

> Let's begin. Sort the pictures into two groups of things that go together. Put one group in box 1. Put the other group in box 2.

Student sorts the cards. Record the response on the class checklist. Use the section labeled **Sorts.** Then point to the objects in each box and say:

> Tell me why these go together. (If needed, give the student a prompt to complete, such as, "All the things are ___.")

Record the responses on the class checklist. Use the section labeled **Classifies.** The most obvious classifications are Toys and Tools. Accept reasonable responses.

Sorting

Sorts and Classifies Objects

Algebra and Functions

EMC 3026 • © Evan-Moor Corp.

Sorts and Classifies Objects

Algebra and Functions

EMC 3026 • © Evan-Moor Corp.

Sorts and Classifies Objects

Algebra and Functions

EMC 3026 • © Evan-Moor Corp.

Sorts and Classifies Objects

Algebra and Functions

EMC 3026 • © Evan-Moor Corp.

Sorts and Classifies Objects

Algebra and Functions

EMC 3026 • © Evan-Moor Corp.

Sorts and Classifies Objects

Algebra and Functions

EMC 3026 • © Evan-Moor Corp.

Sorts and Classifies Objects

Algebra and Functions

EMC 3026 • © Evan-Moor Corp.

Sorts and Classifies Objects

Algebra and Functions

EMC 3026 • © Evan-Moor Corp.

Sorts and Classifies Objects

Algebra and Functions

EMC 3026 • © Evan-Moor Corp.

Sorts and Classifies Objects

Class Checklist	Key:	+ correct response	− incorrect response	• self-corrected

Name	Date	Sorts	Classifies	Notes

Name _____

Make Groups

Cut out the pictures. Glue the things that go together.

Food	Balls

Food

	glue
glue	glue
glue	glue

Balls

	glue
glue	glue

Objective:

Student identifies the object that doesn't belong to a group and classifies the remaining objects.

Materials:

Mat, p. 169

X Card, p. 169

(If you wish, add a tongue depressor to the X card to make for easier handling.)

Class Checklist, p. 171

Activity Sheet, p. 172

Blank sheet of paper

Student Task

Say:

> Today you are going to work with groups of objects.

Place the mat on the table and the X card faceup. Cover all the rows on the mat except row 1 with the sheet of paper. Say:

> Let's begin. Look at row 1. Put the X on what does *not* belong.

Student responds. Record the response on the class checklist. Use the section labeled **Identifies.**

Then point to row 1 and say:

> Why do these go together? (If needed, give the student a prompt to complete, such as, "All the things are ____.")

Record the response in the section labeled **Classifies.** Accept reasonable responses.

Repeat the procedure and the script modeled above for each of the three remaining rows.

Groups

Algebra and Functions
Identifies and Classifies Objects **169**

Identifies and Classifies Objects

Algebra and Functions

EMC 3026 • © Evan-Moor Corp.

**Identifies and
Classifies Objects**
Algebra
and Functions

EMC 3026

© Evan-Moor Corp.

Identifies and Classifies Objects

Class Checklist	Key:	+ correct response	− incorrect response	• self-corrected

Name	Date	Identifies				Classifies				Notes
		Square	3	Balloon	Bird	Row 1	Row 2	Row 3	Row 4	

Name _____

Cross It Out

Make an **X** on what does not belong.

❶
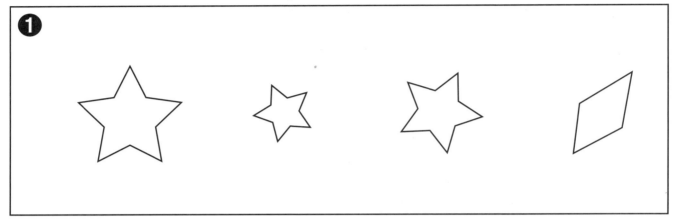

❷
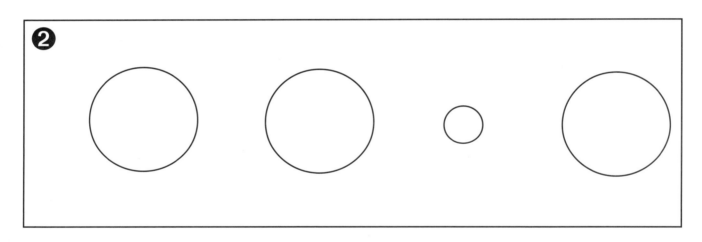

❸

Answer Key

Page 18

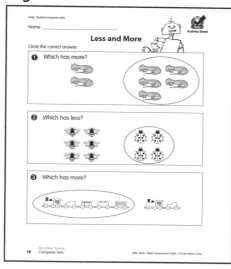

Less and More

Circle the correct answer.

❶ Which has more?

❷ Which has less?

❸ Which has more?

Number Sense
18 Compares Sets   EMC 3026 • Math Assessment Tasks • © Evan-Moor Corp.

Page 22

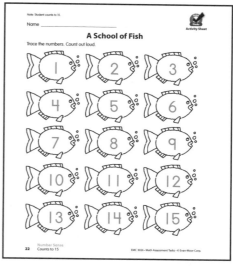

A School of Fish

Trace the numbers. Count out loud.

1   2   3
4   5   6
7   8   9
10 11 12
13 14 15

Number Sense
22 Counts to 15   EMC 3026 • Math Assessment Tasks • © Evan-Moor Corp.

Page 26

Make a Bank

Connect the dots. Count out loud. Start with **1**.

Number Sense
26 Counts to 30   EMC 3026 • Math Assessment Tasks • © Evan-Moor Corp.

Page 34

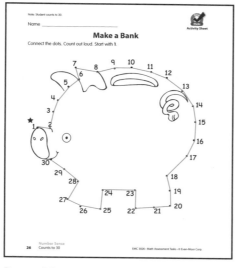

Bugs, Bugs, Bugs

Cut out the bugs. Put the bugs on the pictures. Count out loud.

❶ **2 bugs**

❷ **3 bugs**

❸ **5 bugs**

Number Sense
34 Counts Objects   EMC 3026 • Math Assessment Tasks • © Evan-Moor Corp.

Page 52

Wiggle Worms

Cut out the numbers. Glue them in order.

❶ 1 2 3 4 5 6

❷ 10 11 12 13 14 15

Number Sense
52 Orders Numbers 1 to 15   EMC 3026 • Math Assessment Tasks • © Evan-Moor Corp.

Page 58

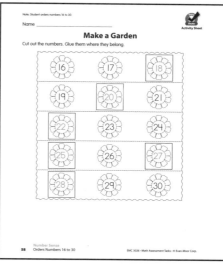

Make a Garden

Cut out the numbers. Glue them where they belong.

16 17 18
19 20 21
22 23 24
25 26 27
28 29 30

Number Sense
58 Orders Numbers 16 to 30   EMC 3026 • Math Assessment Tasks • © Evan-Moor Corp.

Page 64

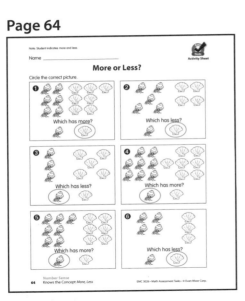

Page 72

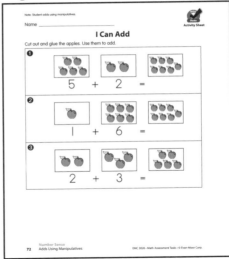

Page 80

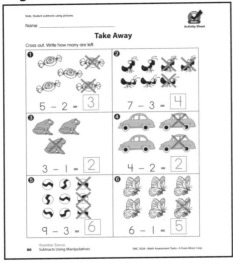

Page 86

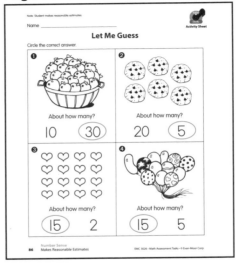

Page 96

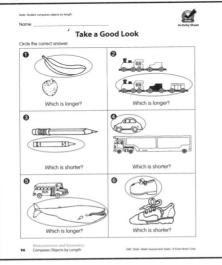

Page 104

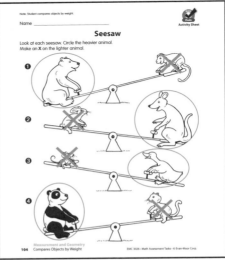

Page 112

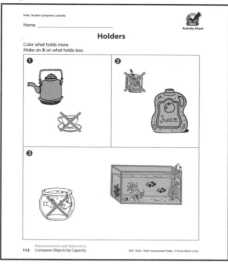

Page 118

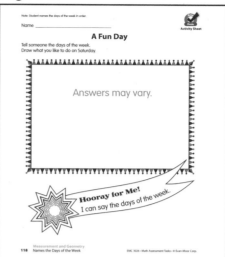

Page 126

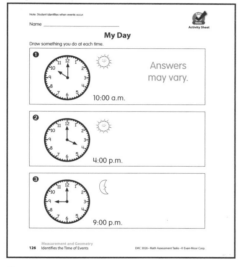

Page 134

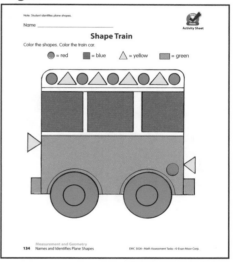

Page 142

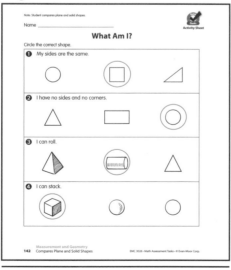

Page 152

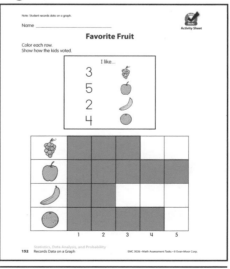

Page 158

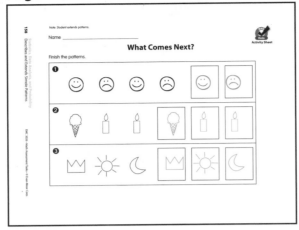

Page 166

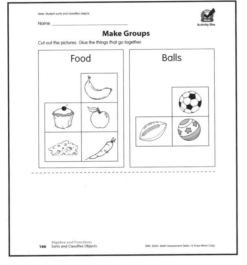

Page 172

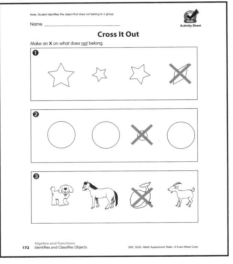